DOES
THIS MEAN
YOU'LL SEE
ME NAKED?

DOES THIS MEAN YOU'LL SEE ME NAKED?

FIELD NOTES FROM A FUNERAL DIRECTOR

ROBERT D. WEBSTER

sourcebooks

Published by Sourcebooks, Inc.
P.O. Box 4410, Naperville, Illinois 60567-4410
(630) 961-3900
Fax: (630) 961-2168
www.sourcebooks.com

Originally published in 2008 by iUniverse Star.

Library of Congress Cataloging-in-Publication Data
Webster, Robert D.
  Does this mean you'll see me naked? : field notes from a funeral director / by Robert
D. Webster.
     p. cm.
  Originally published: Bloomington, IN : IUniverse, 2008.
  1. Undertakers and undertaking—Ohio—Anecdotes, 2. Funeral rites and ceremonies—
Ohio. 3. Funeral homes—Ohio. I. Title.
  HD9999.U53U597 2011
  363.7'5092—dc22
  [B]

                                    2011002336

                Printed and bound in the United States of America.
                       POD 10 9 8 7 6 5 4 3 2

This book is dedicated to my wife, Mel; my daughter, Anna; and my sons, Michael and Ben, for enduring the consequences of my chosen profession. I appreciate the patience afforded me as I was the husband who had to leave the dinner party and the dad who had to exit early from the school play and miss many baseball games over the years because someone's family experienced a death.

⚜ CONTENTS ⚜

ACKNOWLEDGMENTS

MUCH APPRECIATION TO COLLEEN Armstrong, for her push and encouragement to finish this work.

And a special thank-you goes to Cindy Blizzard Browning, for her comment that led to the title of this book.

I ONCE BURIED A pickup truck. I've also handled the funeral plans for 4,500 people, which you'd expect for someone who has more than thirty-three years of experience in the death-care industry. You just might not expect a graveside service for a Ford.

But those of my ilk—and call us what you like: undertakers, embalmers, morticians, funeral directors, or death-care providers—would understand that, unique as it is, this request is all part of a day's work.

I sat down with an elderly man one morning to discuss his funeral plans. The gentleman caught me off guard when he told me he wanted to be buried in the front seat of his Ford pickup truck. When he emphatically assured me that he was not kidding, an amazing discussion occurred.

He had already arranged with a cemetery to purchase two grave spaces to accommodate his truck, a vehicle measuring nineteen feet long and sixty-nine inches wide. He handed me a contract from the cemetery to prove that he had in fact purchased the two graves and a custom-made concrete grave liner, and he pointed out on the contract some specific instructions from the cemetery. That is, the cemetery would honor this unique burial only if the truck was first delivered to a mechanic who would agree to drain all the fluids and remove the battery. After I called a repair shop to obtain such an estimate, we finalized our deal.

The gentleman died a few months later, and I honored his requests. We conducted a visitation and funeral ceremony as usual, with the gentleman reposing in a rental casket. After the funeral service, the pallbearers lifted him out of the casket, and we placed him onto a mortuary cot. The cot was rolled outside to the waiting pickup truck, the pallbearers lifted him into the front seat, and the truck was then pulled up onto a flatbed tow truck. That tow truck, the hearse for the day, led the way in procession to the cemetery. Upon arrival, the pickup truck was lowered to ground level, and then a large construction crane positioned nearby lowered the truck into the grave.

Sometimes it's the request that's unique, but sometimes it's another thing entirely.

My son and I removed one elderly woman from her residence, transported her to the funeral home, and placed her on the preparation room table. We removed her clothing and placed it into a shopping bag to return to the family. When the woman's family arrived, we finalized arrangements and came to the discussion of payment. When I first began my career as a funeral director, I was almost apologetic to bereaved families when discussing the funeral bill. I genuinely felt bad to have to assault them with yet another, perhaps uncomfortable, aspect of the funeral process. After all, it was sobering and sad enough that the family before me had lost their loved one, and I had to tactfully determine whether payment would be forthcoming.

The elderly lady's daughter quickly stopped me mid-sentence to say, "You already have Mom's funeral money."

I was taken aback. Had her mother prearranged and prepaid, and I hadn't found her file? Had she assigned her life insurance to the funeral home already? Was her funeral money in a trust at a bank? Had she transferred a plan from another funeral home to me?

No—it was much less complicated than that.

"You removed Mom's clothes, didn't you?" the daughter asked. "Her funeral money is in her brassiere."

Sure enough, the woman had sewn a pocket inside each cup of her bra and had deposited $3,000 in each side.

The daughter explained that her mother had told her years ago not to worry about her funeral expenses, that she had set aside money for such a purpose. Her mother usually kept the money in a bureau drawer, but as the grandchildren got older and more inquisitive when visiting, she was concerned that some innocent rummaging might reveal her cache. Therefore, she altered her bras, equipping them with pockets to accommodate her stash. The daughter further stated that on several occasions her mother had commented, "Don't forget, my funeral money is right here," and cupped her hands to her chest.

These kinds of things are what really go on after you're dead.

CHAPTER ONE

Why would you want to hang out with dead people?

WHEN THE TELEPHONE RINGS in the middle of the night, my semi-awake mind instantly buzzes into action. Since I have a business phone right next to my bed, and I happen to be a very light sleeper, I have no problem answering and sounding as if I had already been awake for hours. I have discovered that even after thirty years in the funeral business, I don't mind being jolted from sleep.

After I hang up, I sit on the edge of the bed and make a decision. If the death has occurred at a hospital or nursing home, then I will take a shower, get dressed, and get moving. If the death has occurred at a private residence, then I will simply wet down my hair, comb it as well as I can, get dressed, and *really* get moving—a bereaved family is waiting.

The location of the deceased also determines which vehicle I'll use. I can accomplish a hospital or nursing home call with a minivan. A residence requires a hearse. Why? Many years ago, the son of a man who had expired at home was most upset when my assistant and I arrived in a Chevrolet van. As we pulled the mortuary cot out of the back, he exclaimed, horrified, "You came to get my father in a truck?" After that, I resolved never again to attend to a residence call in anything but a hearse.

After working at other funeral homes for more than twenty-five years, I built my own funeral home in 2001, and I have developed my own sense of how I prefer to perform certain tasks. During the drive from my home to the funeral parlor to retrieve the necessary equipment, I make certain observations concerning the call. Does the surname of the deceased sound familiar? Perhaps we have served the family before. Did the family pay their bill the last time? Do I remember anything else about them? Which cemetery did they use? We already have two other deaths this week; which day will these folks request for the funeral?

These and many more thoughts bombard me while on the road in the middle of the night, with only police officers and drunks out there for company. I arrive at the funeral home, greet my assistant, load up the mortuary cot, and off we go. As a teenager, when I assisted my older brother with such duties, he would look over at me as I sat in the passenger seat of our 1968 Cadillac hearse, excited and curious, and he would remark, "And so it begins…" Indeed, it was the start of a long, painful odyssey we would traverse with a grieving family—beginning with the removal of the deceased and ending with the placement of that dead body in its grave.

It's an odyssey that started two centuries ago. The term undertaker was born in the 1800s, when farmers of means discovered that, for a fee, someone was willing to care for their dead. As opposed to those in the immediate household caring for their own deaths in the family, as was the tradition at the time, a family with sufficient resources could call on the local cabinetmaker or wood craftsman to construct a coffin. Whether lacking the necessary carpentry skills or just out of a desire to eliminate such a disheartening task, folks began to reach out to someone independent of the family.

One William Bookbinder, a successful wheat farmer from Coffeyville, Kansas, experienced the death of his beloved wife, Mary. In 1816 Bookbinder traveled to his friend Woodrow Mays, the lumberyard operator in town, and asked Mays whether he would be interested in performing a "grave undertaking" on his behalf. After agreeing on a price for the death care of Mary and the price of the coffin, the use of a wagon and horses, and the digging of the grave, Mays initiated the requested duties. Mays performed his undertaking duties with such tact and proficiency that his fellow townspeople called on him for his specialized services on many more occasions.

Undertaking became a somewhat lucrative sideline for the enterprising businessman of the day. The cabinetmaker and furniture store owner, the dry goods and general store proprietor, and even the livery stable operator all made the transition to undertaker. Cabinetmakers and furniture store purveyors naturally had access to better lumber and the needed craftsmen to build coffins; the dry goods store could provide nice material to line the unadorned box; and the liveryman owned the backboards, wagons, and teams of horses for transportation.

Those cabinetmakers who constructed coffins obviously could not conduct funeral services in their own workshops, however. Livery stable operators who provided horses for funeral carriages could offer little better. So what did American folks in the late 1800s decide to do? They went to church—always a good place for any gathering of mourners. (The unchurched could opt for graveside-only services.) Meanwhile, enterprising undertakers opened storefronts in downtown areas, with their furniture establishments on one side and their funeral parlors right next door. Picture windows facing the street gave passersby an opportunity to view the latest coffins, displayed vertically so that they could inspect the plushest interior options. Since many folks of that era could not read, businesses used symbols, like paintings of horses or horseshoes for the blacksmith or liveryman, for example, or a frothy-headed glass of beer above the swinging doors of the local saloon. The residents of the era recognized the undertaker's establishment as having a picture of a coffin as part of his signage. As more organized and more elaborate funerals came into vogue, undertakers expanded even more by purchasing large, mansionlike homes so that they could live upstairs and conduct business downstairs.

When the automobile arrived in the early 1900s, leading undertakers immediately seized the advantage. A motorized hearse to carry a casket to the cemetery was a source of immense pride and fueled competitive fires among many funeral parlors. Another potential source of revenue soon galloped into mind: Why not use the hearse for an ambulance on occasions when the funeral business was slow? The infirm could be transported to the hospital for treatment and then return home in a fine conveyance—complete with the undertaker's name emblazoned on that vehicle's sides. When Grandma eventually died, which firm do you think the family called to conduct her funeral service? It was definitely a win-win situation.

Ambulance services became such a staple in the funeral industry that major hearse manufacturers were soon building what they termed *combinations*. A hearse-ambulance on a Cadillac chassis had reversible rollers in the rear casket compartment. The rollers allowed for a casket to slide into the rear of the hearse, yet they could also disappear into the floor to easily accommodate an ambulance cot. Anyone who has ever attended a funeral will instantly recognize the genius behind this concept.

In just a few short years, the undertaker would be introduced to the greatest innovative technique—one that changed the funeral business from a mere sideline to the professional and respected industry we know today:

embalming. You might think it's the selection of fine coffins, and other impressive undertaking equipment, yet none of that matters if the deceased human remains rotting in that fine coffin.

The funeral business is about the body. In the early undertaker's day, the body was the focal point, not the coffin or the undertaker's caring attitude. Today, though, much is made about the great strides achieved in casket design and innovation, funeral home amenities, and after-care provided to bereaved families. All of that is well and good, yet today more than ever, the dead human body should be the ultimate focus of the funeral industry.

So why on earth would anyone want to work with dead people in the first place? I have been asked that question more times than I can count.

Actually, working with the deceased is probably the smallest facet of the entire funeral process. Far more time and attention are spent with the bereaved family. So I'll simply repeat what funeral directors in the United States have been telling the public for nearly two hundred years: I provide a very essential and valuable service. In that regard, what I do for a living is a mere step away from practicing medicine, teaching first grade, or hoisting a fire hose. Undertakers are as devoted to helping people in need as people in those other professions.

The older I become, the more I realize how important that role is, especially when I see so much pain in the eyes of surviving family members. My taking charge becomes even more vital when I am acquainted with or personally related to the deceased. Once I dealt with the deaths of my classmates' grandparents, and now I am caring for their parents. Although I certainly dislike facing close friends who have lost loved ones, I also know that most are very pleased that their undertaker is someone they know.

I was tested severely, however, in 1992, when my niece, still in her twenties, tragically lost her husband. The two were newlyweds, the handsomest of couples. My niece was summoned to the hospital, unaware that her husband was already dead. She arrived, assuming that he had merely injured himself on the job.

When informed of her husband's death, she was asked which funeral home she preferred. Still devastated, she told the nurse, "You'll have to call my uncle, Bob Webster." Upon my arrival at the hospital, my niece was visibly relieved that a family member would handle things. That tragic death left a mark on me that endures to this day— but although she was heartbroken, I was glad to offer some small degree of comfort.

The same thoughts returned recently when the thirty-six-year-old son of a close friend died. My friend is an upbeat, caring gentleman who always greets my children with huge, heartfelt bear hugs. Although reluctant to face him at such a horrible time, I was gratified when he told me that he would not have allowed anyone else to handle the funeral arrangements. He was reassured, knowing that I would treat his son and family just as I would my own.

Despite these stories, the general public continues to respond to what I do with morbid fascination. Overall, I think I'm a pretty normal guy. I go to parties. I enjoy baseball and backyard barbecuing. I tell lots of corny jokes—just ask my kids. I don't wear a black cape. I don't have fangs or talons.

I believe that hang-ups about funeral directors have much to do with our culture's obsession with youth, beauty, fitness—all that means a total denial of death. The acknowledgment that we funeral directors exist and can over time earn a substantial living confronts everyone with the jarring, indisputable evidence that—oh my gosh!— people die.

That they do, every day. And that's where I come in. These are my stories.

CHAPTER TWO

Does this mean you'll see me naked?

YES, IT DOES MEAN precisely that. The funeral director who prepares your body for a final viewing will invariably at some point need to remove your clothing. So, yes. You will be naked.

But you'd be amazed at how many times I've been asked that question—and how often, when people voice their fears regarding death, the issue comes up. What is this hang-up people have about nudity? It's as bad as their hang-up about death! Some of my closest friends have expressed reservations in letting me handle their funerals because of it; even my own sister has mentioned it!

I have repeatedly assured everyone that, as a professional, I have no sexual interest whatsoever in dead bodies—male or female—particularly family members and friends. Any loved one reposing on my embalming table is someone's mother, father, sister, brother, daughter, son, or grandparent and is reverently and respectfully cared for in a totally businesslike manner. Only a sick mind would interpret or insinuate anything else.

Furthermore, preparation room decorum has always been maintained wherever I have worked. All of my coworkers have been men, and in my opinion, men are all pretty much mama's boys. They therefore reserve a great deal of respect for deceased women. Any little old lady reminds them of their own beloved grandmothers; a middle-aged woman might be the same age as their mothers. And in the case of a deceased little girl, all of us are instantly transformed into protective father figures, feeling intense sorrow right along with the family and sometimes even blubbering in tears as we work.

There have obviously been cases involving improprieties in funeral home settings, but such incidents are few and far between. Many years ago I worked at a home with a man who eagerly reported for work each morning and then made a mad dash to the preparation room to see whether there had been any calls overnight—he supposedly wanted to see whether he knew the recently deceased personally. If so, he was on the horn immediately to report the death to his wife and other acquaintances. But he also made a habit of lifting the sheets covering deceased women so that he could gaze at their private areas. When I questioned him one day, he responded that he was merely looking for a toe tag to determine identity. "The tag is not in her crotch," I told him. He sheepishly left. But when the same incident occurred again the next morning, I reported him to my immediate supervisor. The man was fired on the spot, and rightfully so.

BODY ART

Sometimes we funeral directors do occasionally marvel at the physical oddities we encounter. As a college student working in the county morgue, I saw several decedents whose attributes were, well, noteworthy. Some took the form of off-the-wall embellishments.

A navy man lay on the table one morning; he sported tattoos over nearly every inch of his body, save for his hands and face. A detailed battleship, complete with billowing smokestacks, festooned his chest. On his back, from neck to buttocks, was an intricately designed butterfly. Around his neck was a broken line with the words *Cut Here* in bold letters. The stereotypical *Mom* was emblazoned on each bicep, and on each forearm was a buxom lady, each one naked and well endowed. On each leg, from groin to ankle, were hissing snakes with open mouths and forked tongues. And, of course, he had the prerequisite *love* on his four left fingers and *hate* on the four right ones. (All such body art is considered a distinguishing mark and is therefore noted and photographed by morgue personnel.)

I entered the morgue another day to find the coroner holding a magnifying glass to the private parts of a naked man. As I stood next to the body, the coroner handed me the magnifying glass and told me to check out the head of the man's penis. In full detail was a tattoo of a housefly.

A few months later, we used the magnifying glass again to observe another penis tattoo, this one reading *Cherry Buster*. I had to wonder just how drunk that person must have been when he decided to get that tattoo. Perhaps the finest tattoo I have seen to date, though, is a red-and-white barber pole design, no doubt meant to resemble a candy cane.

Tattoos on deceased women are usually less brazen—flowers, butterflies, and the occasional Harley-Davidson insignia. However, I've also encountered *Jimmy's Toys* emblazoned above a woman's ample breasts; *Honey Pot*, complete with an elaborate arrow directing the viewer to the vaginal area; and most incredibly, *Deliveries in Rear* inscribed just above a young lady's buttocks.

Back when I got started, there were not many piercings of note, unlike today. Now men have rings attached to their penises and scrota, women have rings in their clitorises, and both males and females sport nipple rings. Among the more elaborate piercings I've seen was that of a young woman who had both nipples and her clitoris pierced, and all three were connected. A gold chain attached to her nipples hung downward in a *U* shape across her chest with another chain attaching the center of the nipple chain to the ring located between her legs. When her mother asked me for any jewelry her daughter might have been wearing, I nervously explained my findings. Although upset, she graciously accepted the items following the funeral.

FACE DOWN AND NAKED

In my business, prurience, or at least the suggestion of it, is an ongoing issue. I once prearranged the funeral services of a man who insisted that he be placed in his casket completely naked and face down. At first I assumed that this was his interpretation of the old cliché, "Lay me out face down and naked, so the whole world can kiss my ass."

However, his explanation was far less dramatic. He'd always slept on his stomach and in the nude, he said, and he desired to be positioned that very way for burial. Also, his casket should be closed, for obvious reasons. I drew red asterisks all over the front of his prearrangement sheet, so that in case I was away when this gentleman passed on, others would be aware of his wishes.

When he died two years later, I informed his daughter of his request, and she readily agreed to it. I placed the man on a dressing table, covered him with a sheet, and then allowed the daughter to view her father and say good-bye before proceeding with the aforementioned arrangements.

Honoring requests of the deceased is something we pride ourselves on, and those requests take many forms. Many family members have expressed to me that their deceased loved one would have enjoyed a less-than-traditional send-off—more of a party atmosphere than the normal visitation and ceremony complete with traditional hymns and a consoling sermon from a man of the cloth. Although many mention a desire to do something different, I can think of very few who have actually carried out such a plan.

There was one memorable one, however. Twenty years ago, I arranged for a visitation and service to be held in the social room of an exclusive retirement center. The facility was ahead of its time, without peer. Separate condominium-like housing was available for those who were still active and could drive their own cars, and there were also assisted living areas and a nursing home setting. The gentleman who had passed away was a wealthy business owner. His three grown children applauded his zest for life and preference for the finer trappings. His oldest son told me that his father always wanted to have a send-off that involved his Dixieland bandmates, with whom he had played for many years. They had marched on the field at Cincinnati Reds and Bengals games, and the group had remained quite close into their old age.

So the social room at the retirement community was bedecked not with black bunting but with bright green ribbons and noisemakers normally reserved for New Year's Eve. The kitchen staff strolled around with serving trays, offering finger food and alcoholic beverages. I stood at the room's rear, pleased by what I observed—folks of all ages eating, drinking, and toasting the deceased. Here was the life of the party, the one they'd all come to honor, lying in a solid bronze casket, dressed in a pair of black tuxedo trousers, a white ruffled shirt, green satin bow tie, and a red-and-white striped sports jacket. His bandmates were off to one side loudly playing "Sweet Georgia Brown" and having the time of their lives. When the band took a break, they all congregated at their late friend's casket, each tipping a glass in his honor.

The deceased man had left behind a wife and a wealth of memories, especially from their annual trip to Hawaii. At the funeral the next day, in recognition of his love for our fiftieth state, I was asked to play the music of Don Ho. His favorite song? "Tiny Bubbles." Everyone in attendance received a small bottle of soap bubbles and the obligatory wand. As the mourners and family members passed the casket, they administered a bubbly tribute as the song wafted in the background.

Sometimes, associates of the deceased attempt to honor certain requests without considering the presence and possible opposition of family members. A motorcycle gang once approached me at a visitation and ordered me to take their late friend out of his casket and place him onto a chapel sofa so that he would appear to be relaxing with his buddies. I refused—and amazingly I had to explain to this band of drunks that perhaps the man's parents and grandparents might take offense. The group's mouthpiece adamantly claimed that the deceased had always insisted that he did not want to be in a casket for his visitation and asked me to place him on the couch immediately. After a few more minutes of explanations, the others finally conceded my point, apparently realizing how disrespectful such a move would have been.

Disrespect can take many forms. A young man killed in an auto accident reposed in his casket with gospel hymns playing softly in the background. His parents were very religious and appreciated the solemnity of Christian music for a churchlike atmosphere. But the decedent's hoodlum friends requested that I instead play the rap CDs they had brought along. I looked over the cases and discovered warnings proclaiming that the talentless ramblings contained extremely explicit, profane, and sexually degrading lyrics, obviously inappropriate for a funeral. I showed the CDs to the parents, and to my surprise, they said to go ahead and play them. Well, after about three minutes into the first selection, the father frantically begged me to go back to the hymns. He and his family had probably never heard the bittersweet recollections of a "ho" shaking "the junk in her trunk" and feverishly fondling many male appendages until they "shot their spunk."

When a fun-loving seventy-year-old attorney died, his widow expressed to me his desire to have no minister present. One of her late husband's law firm partners would officiate at the funeral instead. Once everyone was seated in the chapel, I escorted the speaker to the podium, noting that he had clearly had a few too many martinis. Not overly concerned, though, I took my position outside the chapel doors to watch the ceremony on a closed-circuit television screen.

What I saw and heard was most amazing. This fellow began the ceremony with offensive jokes about Jews, blacks, homosexuals, and Mexicans. It turned out that this was the daily water-cooler banter of the deceased and his colleagues; therefore, such material was deemed perfectly appropriate for his funeral. His widow did not even seem offended. Quite a few attendees, however, succumbed to embarrassment and departed, red-faced, through the rear chapel door. Many more left in disgust as the speaker began an X-rated appreciation of various female attributes.

Bury Me with Buster

Honoring last requests is often a simple matter of inclusion. Over the years I have placed myriad items inside caskets—fishing rods, a bow and arrow, golf clubs (sometimes a whole set), golf balls, basketballs, autographed baseballs, baseball gloves, and other sports memorabilia, along with complete baseball, football, and basketball uniforms. Unloaded handguns, rifles, and shotguns often find their way into the casket—sometimes because the deceased was an avid hunter, but just as often because someone apparently didn't want certain family members to take possession. I've included playing cards, bingo cards, lucky pennies, room keys from hotels in Las Vegas and other destinations, cigarettes, marijuana joints, pet rocks, favorite books, a tape recorder, a glass eye, sexual devices, jewelry (some expensive, some not), apples, oranges, buckeyes, walnuts, photographs, leaf collections, coin collections, *Penthouse* and *Playboy* magazines (once, an entire collection), and occasionally even a racier publication.

Then there are the dead animals—cremated remains of

beloved dogs and cats or the recently euthanized dog, which is placed in a plastic bag and laid at the feet of the deceased.

One recent casket-depositing incident caused quite a furor. The late gentleman was thrice married and divorced, and all three of his ex-spouses insisted on attending the services. His current female companion abruptly requested that I remove one of those ex-wives from the funeral home as soon as possible. "Why?" I inquired. She informed me that the woman had just peeled off her panties and placed them in her late ex-husband's hand.

The majority of gestures are loving, however. An elderly gentleman friend contacted me when his wife passed away. After the service and with the room empty of mourners, he and I approached the casket. He then handed me a $50 bill and requested that I slip it into his wife's bra. Apparently it was a tradition of sorts—whenever she went someplace without him, he would playfully slip $50 into her bra so she would always have some money with her. This time would be no exception.

CHAPTER THREE

Moving the body

IN MOST CASES, THE deceased human body is not the most pleasant sight to behold. Immediately after death, many changes begin to take place: discoloration, bowel and bladder evacuations, drainage from the mouth and nose.

Only once can I recall a time when a dead body was actually good looking. On Christmas Day, 1978, I was called to a newly constructed apartment complex to remove a twenty-four-year-old suicide victim. A young woman, apparently distraught over a recent breakup with her boyfriend, had hung herself in a clothes closet. This was long before *CSI*, *Cold Case Files*, and Drs. Henry Lee and Michael Baden. So the responding life-squad personnel cut the woman down and laid her on the bed, coincidentally just as a funeral director would—on her back, a pillow under her head, legs together, and hands across her abdomen, left over right.

They had called the coroner, but he did not respond—it was 1978, remember. He simply phoned me and verbally released the body. Since there would be no autopsy, I could make the removal immediately.

The figure lying on the bed was at first breathtaking. She resembled Marilyn Monroe, and her breasts protruded straight upward from her chest like twin Mt. Fujis. There was no droop to one side, which is normal in death. There was no sheet covering her, because life-squad personnel and the police photographer were as utterly stunned as I was. The only other woman in the room was a paramedic. She touched them and testified that those breasts were indeed not God given but saline implants. I had never heard of such a thing. By 1970s standards, this young woman was something of a trendsetter.

A closer examination of her body revealed that, except for her breasts, there were the usual damning influences of death—her mouth and nose were full of foamy lung material; a deep, ear-to-ear gash reddened under her chin from her ligature of choice (a Venetian-blind cord), and the increasingly pungent odor of body wastes filled the room. So much for beauty. So much for leaving a good-looking corpse, as the actor John Derek said in the film *Knock on Any Door*. Within moments of death, that's usually an impossibility.

DEATH BY DEFECATION

I learned another valuable lesson once when removing a nude, deceased man from his second-floor bathroom:

There are never enough linens on a mortuary cot. The man in question had just drawn a bath and was sitting on the toilet. He died while he was still on the commode.

My assistant and I draped a bed sheet across the bathroom floor, then placed the decedent on the sheet and wrapped it around him. We had left our mortuary cot at the foot of the stairs near the front door, since it was not possible to carry it up to the bathroom. We began to hoist the decedent to move him downstairs. My assistant's left arm was under the nape of the man's neck to support his head. His right arm was under the small of his back. I had placed my left arm there, too, with my right arm under his knees. As we made our descent down the stairs, I felt a warm sensation on my thigh, followed by more warmth on the top of my right foot, accompanied by a familiar odor. I strained against the weight in my arms in an attempt to discover the source. Just as I suspected, the decedent's bowels had given way in a shower of feces that trailed all the way down the carpeted steps and all over our pants and feet.

After placing the decedent on the mortuary cot, I asked the family if I might use their telephone. I called several carpet-cleaning companies and ultimately reached one that would come to the residence right away. Of course, I paid the carpet cleaner myself, still resplendent in my odiferous attire. But from then on, I always made certain I brought an extra three or four sheets along with the cot. If we had wrapped the man in several sheets, rather than just one, the problem would have easily been contained within the linens. And in most situations, people normally are wearing some sort of clothing, at least pajamas or underwear.

A house call to remove a decedent from a private residence, as opposed to a medical facility, often involves entering the person's bathroom. Such scenarios used to dumbfound me. However, an obvious case can be made in that the elderly sometimes experience difficulty with their bowel movements, and the inherent strain may be a contributing factor in their deaths. We call it "death by defecation."

Many years ago, the county coroner summoned me to a residence. As I wrote down the street and house number, it sounded very familiar. Once I turned onto the street, I realized that I was on my way to the home of a kindly old minister friend. Over the years, I had driven to his house several times to take him to the funeral home to preside over services.

As I pulled in front, I noted an ambulance parked nearby. The EMTs and two police officers stood on the minister's porch smoking cigarettes, waiting for me to arrive. Everybody smoked back then, so usually we all lit up and discussed our plan for removing the body. But the assembled group appeared to be sizing me up. I quickly discovered why. It seems that my friend had expired while perched on the commode, and he had subsequently slumped against the door of the tiny bathroom, his full weight pressing it closed.

We all ventured inside to allow me to survey the situation and offer my expert evaluation of possible procedures. The EMTs and police officers decided that, since I was the skinniest one present and familiar with the decedent, I should be the one to climb inside a small window, squeeze my way into the tiny bathroom, move the man away from the interior door, and thus allow for proper removal.

I took off my fairly new, double-knit suit coat and, with some assistance, delivered myself into the bathroom through a window never designed for a six-foot-three man. In those days, I was agile enough to stick my left leg into the room first, and then swing my right leg and stand upright without even banging my head on the upper window frame.

I was certainly saddened to see my friend deceased— but also to encounter him in such a state. He still held a *Newsweek* magazine, clutched in his motionless right hand. I have since removed many decedents from bathrooms, but more often they are lying on the floor. However, it is not uncommon to have to pluck a person from atop a commode and then place him on a mortuary cot.

Still, a house call (when death occurs at a private residence) tests the strength and sometimes the ingenuity of those doing the removal. A ranch-style home or any residence in which the deceased is located on the ground level is a huge plus. In at least half the cases I encounter, however, my hopes are dashed when I learn the person is on the second or third floor.

New home construction considers not the lowly funeral director. Wide doorways and high-ceilinged atria in the living areas often give way to narrow upstairs hallways and doorways barely wide enough for a mortuary cot, let alone an ambulance gurney. People should keep this in mind—they're likely to need ambulances long before they need funeral directors.

Long ago, when I was a young and foolish teenager, I assisted my older brother, then also a budding funeral director, on several occasions to run ambulance calls and make removals. One morning we were called to the home of a wealthy family. The homeowner's drunken black sheep of a brother had died on the mansion's third floor. So we left our cot near the front door (it weighs nearly one hundred pounds and is difficult to maneuver to higher floors) and clambered up the steps to survey the situation. We had brought with us a collapsible device called a litter, which is basically three steel poles supporting a thick canvas sheet, and commonly used to traverse stairs.

On entering the room, we discovered the 350-pound decedent supine on the hardwood floor, clad only in jockey shorts and a T-shirt—which was thoroughly soaked in vomit. His stomach contents puddled around the entire body. I had never witnessed such a thing, and I was on the verge of involuntarily giving up the ham sandwich I had consumed only a half hour earlier.

We placed the litter on the floor next to the deceased, and my older, wiser brother began to rattle off the game plan: I was to simultaneously take hold of the thin T-shirt and the waistband of the jockey shorts and then turn his body toward myself as my brother pushed the litter beneath him. A good-sounding plan—except that I was barely able to budge him. Plan B entailed both of us lifting the man onto the litter by brute force. Again, I was to grasp the T-shirt and my brother, the waistband.

But this plan went awry as the thin, vomit-soaked shirt slipped from my grasp, and the deceased hit the hardwood floor with a resounding thud. Family members downstairs no doubt heard the commotion, but we hoped they thought we had knocked over a chair. Immaturity ruled as both my brother and I nearly collapsed in fits of muffled laughter, to the point that both of our young faces were red with shame.

On our second try, we were finally able to position the deceased on the litter, cover him, and make our lumbering way down the steps to the waiting cot. Our faces still red, we prayed that the family would assume that our strenuous trek down the stairs with a 350-pound man in tow was the source of our breathlessness.

THE TIME OF DEATH IS...

These days family members are often present even when a death occurs outside the home, such as at a nursing facility or even a hospital. In the past, when I arrived at a nursing home at three o'clock in the morning, no one but the nurse on duty was available to help move the deceased out of the bed and onto the cot. Today the family is often waiting—I suppose because nursing home caregivers attend death education classes that stress that family members should be at a terminal patient's bedside for end-of-life support. At hospitals this can be more complicated, because most hospitals still require that hospital personnel transport the deceased to the facility's morgue, where the body is left in cold storage until the funeral director arrives.

With the hospice movement having become so popular, however, more and more terminally ill people are choosing to die in their own homes or in those of family members, as opposed to in the antiseptic settings of hospital rooms. Hospice nurses and other caregivers are usually present when such a death occurs, or they are quickly summoned if needed. A death in hospice care at a private residence is not considered "death without medical attendance." For example, when someone is found deceased at home and not under hospice care, the coroner or medical examiner almost always will examine the case. Some counties require a pronouncement of death by a physician. On many occasions I have had to transport a deceased loved one from his or her place of residence to a hospital, so that one of the doctors on duty could come out to the transport vehicle and pronounce the patient dead. Nine times out of ten, the doctor looks briefly at the deceased and then at his or her wristwatch and says, "Let's call it 2:45 a.m." That is declared the official time of death, even though the patient more than likely expired an hour or so earlier.

Very rarely do doctors come out to a funeral home vehicle completely equipped to make a death pronouncement—no flashlight to shine into the eyes and no stethoscope to detect a heartbeat.

It is important, though, to make sure that the patient is actually dead! I have heard of cases of nursing home patients being transported to funeral homes only to "come to life" during the trip. A colleague once told me that he had an elderly man on his preparation room table and was in the process of removing the man's clothing when the "dead" man suddenly began to moan and move. After a few seconds of freaking out, my colleague called for an ambulance. The old man was very much alive; he was transferred to a hospital to stay overnight and the next day he returned to the nursing home.

Sometimes I have been just about to roll up the cot to the wrong bed in a nursing home, only to hear the person still breathing. Obviously, I needed to attend the bedside of his or her late roommate. At some older nursing homes, patients are bedded in wards, and there are three or four non-ambulatory people in one large room, which is separated into sections by a floor-to-ceiling privacy curtain. Arriving in the dark in the middle of the night, a kindly nurse in charge once commented to me, "Take your pick," as we surveyed a row of four elderly patients, all of whom appeared to be dead.

Before the invention of the stethoscope, there were some interesting tests for death. The fire test involved holding an open flame to the skin of the potentially deceased. If the skin blistered, then the patient was not dead—skin cannot blister after death. For the mirror test, a small handheld mirror was positioned under the nose or mouth. If the mirror fogged, then there was obviously breath. The water test was administered by placing a glass of water on the chest to detect any motion in the water from the rise and fall of breathing.

Even such fail-safe tests were not trustworthy; that is why the term *wake* came to be. Today a wake is a visitation period for offering sympathy and support, but originally a wake involved staying awake with the deceased to make sure he or she was in fact dead. If a moan, a twitch, or any other movement took place, then obviously the person was still alive. I imagine such things occurred quite frequently in the late 1800s and early 1900s, when a comatose patient or even someone who had fainted was often assumed to be deceased.

INSIDE THE AUTOPSY

An autopsy may be required for medical or legal reasons—suspected homicide, accident, suicide, or other probable unnatural death. Many teaching hospitals, such as those with a degreed nursing program, or hospitals owned and operated by a university, are required by hospital associations to conduct a certain number of autopsies for teaching purposes.

As an orderly during my college days, I witnessed hundreds of autopsies. As a result, I fervently hope that such a procedure is never performed on anyone in my family. Before proceeding, the pathologist would hand me a notepad and pencil, both already stained with blood from his earlier notations on height, weight, and general appearance. I was the designated stenographer, assigned to note the weight and condition of each organ and any abnormalities detected. I perused the initial notations of the pathologist so that I could be equally descriptive—I didn't want to appear inexperienced. Standard initial commentary was already present: "A fifty-four-year-old white female, eyes brown in color, natural hair, streaked in gray. Well nourished, with all natural teeth present. Surgical scar on abdomen suggests past hysterectomy, with no other scars or anomalies noted."

First, a *Y* incision is made with a scalpel on the chest of the decedent. A large knife pares away the muscle and fatty tissue to expose the ribs. The ribs are cut away with a cast saw to expose the thoracic and abdominal organs for the pathologist's inspection.

The initial sight of exposed human organs always takes everyone aback. My first glimpse reassured me that there is a God, because all of those organs must work together in perfect synchronization to sustain life, and that's something so complex that only God could make it possible.

After the initial reaction to the sight comes the shock of odor. Blood reeks after death, as do stomach contents and the contents of the colon. Then you note the vivid colors of human organs: the mottled, black-specked appearance of a lung; the reddish-purple hue of a heart; the grayish-blue tint and the glistening wet appearance of a kidney; the three-lobed liver the color of any calf liver in a super-market meat case.

The pathologist then used a large knife to open the pericardial sac, the structure that surrounds the heart. With a qualified, deft slice, he released the heart from its moorings. The dripping heart was placed in a stainless-steel basket attached to a ceiling-mounted scale. The heart's weight is critical; if a heart is heavier than normal, that's an obvious red flag and probably the cause of death. An enlarged, and heavier, heart sometimes pinches off the nearby arteries, dramatically decreasing the blood flow.

After being weighed, the heart was placed on a cutting board, where the pathologist sectioned it to meticulously search for any abnormality, such as scars from past or recent coronary disease.

The remaining organs were removed and examined in the same fashion, with a few exceptions. The stomach was removed and the contents poured into a stainless-steel container for inspection. The first time I witnessed this procedure I was close to nausea. Stomach acids that had ceased working nonetheless carried the familiar odor of vomit. Certain foods do not digest quickly. Salad greens, broccoli, and baked potato skins are clearly recognizable among stomach contents, as are drug capsule remains. I was once instructed to use a screened ladle, much like a net used in fishbowls, to dip into the stomach of a patient who had potentially ingested many chloral hydrate capsules to commit suicide. It was amazing to know the death was on purpose, which I knew as soon as I scooped out more than forty capsules, some dissolved but some very recognizable.

Probably the most unpleasant part of an autopsy is the procedure called *running chitlins*: several feet of intestines curled up in the abdomen are pulled out a foot or so at a time by an assistant (me) and then handed to the pathologist, who slices open the structures and inspects the interiors for tumors, restrictions, or any other abnormalities. Part of my duty was also to squeeze the exterior of the intestine to force fecal material out of the way so the pathologist could obtain a clearer view. That particular procedure took a little getting used to, but after a few times, I thought nothing of it.

After witnessing many autopsies, all the sights and smells became commonplace. When I became a seasoned veteran, I have to admit that I enjoyed watching young nursing students entering the autopsy theater for the first time. Standing four across at the head of the autopsy table, the fresh-faced kids all wore looks of frightened anticipation. Once the scalpel made the first cut, and the body opened up in all its glory, the students' countenances changed from nervous grins and smirks to mouth-dropping stares and curled upper lips.

Death unmasks us all.

CHAPTER FOUR

The morbidly obese

MORBIDLY OBESE DECEDENTS POSE some special challenges. Let me be clear in the beginning—I mean no disrespect to any folks who carry excess weight. But given that the death care of the morbidly obese occurs more frequently today than ever, so much so that casket companies now offer a specific line of caskets reserved for that increasing niche of decedents, talking about how we delicately handle these situations can shed some light on the state of death care.

For example, several years ago, I was called to the residence of a deceased thirty-five-year-old female who weighed 660 pounds. Luckily, the local fire department was already on the scene—the firefighters had dealt with the woman's medical problems before and knew the inherent problems of transporting her. She was found face-up in bed ("bed" was two twin-sized mattresses on two-inch sheets of plywood that had been glued together and were supported at each corner by concrete blocks). After reviewing the situation, I took the mortuary cot out of the hearse and left it in her front yard. There would be no way she could fit on something that was only twenty-two inches wide. The life-squad personnel and I pondered our dilemma for a few moments. Then I came up with the plan of the century.

I drove to a nearby hardware store to purchase a large canvas tarpaulin to spread out on the floor next to the woman's bed. Seven men assisted me in grasping the bed linens beneath her and gently pulling her onto the tarp. With four of us on each side, we gripped the tarp and slowly moved her to the front door and into the hearse.

That was the first time I ever placed a body directly on the floor of a hearse, and there was little room to spare. I asked the life-squad personnel to follow me back to the funeral home so they could help me transfer her into the building. At the funeral home, I had to make some adjustments: because the decedent was forty-three inches wide, she couldn't possibly fit onto a standard embalming table. I placed two tables side by side and latched them together at the legs with nylon rope. The eight of us took baby steps with the tarp and its cargo into the funeral home, down a short hallway, and into the preparation room. Then, after a brief rest, we counted to three and hoisted the decedent onto the joined embalming tables.

Later, since I could not hold the mass of fatty tissue away from her neck to locate the carotid artery or jugular vein, I opted to find and raise the right femoral artery and vein, located in the upper thigh near the groin. After making the femoral incision, I had to ask an assistant to hold open the incision with his hands and some strategically placed duct tape. I was nearly up to my elbow in fatty tissue before I finally could delve deep enough in the femoral space to locate the selected vessels. Arterially embalming a decedent of average weight usually consumes from three to five gallons of formaldehyde-based chemical. In this case, I injected fourteen gallons through the decedent's arterial system before I finally started recognizing some positive results.

When I received her burial clothing the next day, I pondered the sheer size of the black dress she was to be buried in. My wife styled her hair, I applied cosmetics, and we awaited the arrival of my seven assistants to move the woman into her substantial casket. I had ordered a custom-made forty-five-inch-wide, eighteen-gauge steel version, which had been delivered that day.

The next hurdle was coming up with a proper device on which to place the casket. A standard bier, a wooden pedestal-like device on wheels, would not be strong enough to support her weight. I called around to inquire about the price of having a special bier constructed on short notice—but to no avail. During one fruitless call, however, a gentleman referred me to a welding shop known to have rolling carts on which they mounted equipment. The owner invited me to come over and take a look at a steel cart that sported heavy-duty steel wheels. He agreed to deliver the cart to me, and after a good scrubbing and applying black bunting around the top edge, it was perfectly serviceable.

Throughout the entire process, I made one serious blunder. I had placed the casket on the floor of the preparation room and removed the lid, so that we could get around both sides as we lifted it. Removing the lid was an excellent idea; laying the casket on the floor was not. We hoisted the decedent into her casket and positioned her as well as possible so that she would look comfortable in her repose. But that's when my blunder sank in. We would need to lift her again—this time with the added weight of the casket in which she was lying! I apologized to my hoisting partners and admitted that I should have placed the empty casket into position on the welding cart and then situated the decedent. I also vowed never to make such a mistake again.

Since a forty-three-inch-wide casket will not fit into a hearse, a standard burial vault, or standard grave, I had to devise a mode of transportation to the cemetery and then arrange for oversize accommodations there. The burial vault company offered its flatbed truck, which was also equipped with a hydraulic crane, for use as a hearse. Following the funeral, the truck backed up to the chapel door, and two canvas-strap slings were slid underneath the casket. With little strain, the hydraulic lift gently swooped the casket onto the truck for its short journey to the cemetery.

I'm sure the sight of a white flatbed truck with a very large blue casket on the back leading a funeral procession down the street is not very common. When we arrived at the cemetery, I noticed that an inordinate number of gawkers had staked their claims near the grave site to catch a glimpse of what they had heard was a woman with a very large casket.

The bottom part of the vault was twice the normal size. The vault company also made concrete septic tanks, so with such a large grave opening, it had used an actual septic tank. For the first time, I witnessed a graveside ceremony standing next to a minister and a vault truck, with the honored decedent resting on the truck's bed rather than on a lowering device above the open grave. With a twist of a lever, the casket was raised and gently cranked down to its final resting place.

CASKET TECH

Expensive caskets, such as those of sixteen-gauge steel, stainless steel, solid copper, and solid bronze, are sometimes urn shaped rather than rectangular. The urn shape is not only more attractive and more expensive but also serves a practical purpose for funeral directors. The extra inch or so of width inside allows us to position a heavier person in a more comfortable repose. With arms crossed across the abdomen, the elbows rest against the interior sides of the casket. Without that extra room, the deceased appears, and is, stuffed uncomfortably into the casket.

For decedents who weigh 350 pounds and up, oversize caskets must be used. A standard casket's interior dimensions are twenty-three inches wide and seventy-eight inches long. Oversize caskets are available in widths of twenty-seven, thirty, and thirty-four inches. For the morbidly obese, custom-made caskets must be specially manufactured and are usually available in two or three days.

Many midrange and high-end caskets are equipped with a plastic tray underneath the dead body—a fail-safe liner. Embalming and other fluids frequently ooze from the deceased even if an expert and thorough embalming job has been done. Incisions that have not dried properly or have not been stitched tightly enough have also been known to leak, as does the site of the trocar, where embalmers insert a thin, tube-like instrument just above the belly button to aspirate the thoracic and abdominal cavities. Obese decedents present an additional problem in this regard because of the immense pressure on the abdomen from their weight and the weight of their arms and hands resting on the belly.

Many years ago I was approached at a visitation by the deceased's spouse, whose husband was morbidly obese. She asked me to explain the moisture and the odd sound emanating from his casket. Luckily, he was dressed in a black sports shirt, which made the moisture less apparent to the public; however, as I held my ear to his belly, I could distinguish a bass sound similar to the opening notes of the 1960s gag song "Tie Me Kangaroo Down Sport." I asked those gathered to leave the room for a moment while I investigated further.

I pulled up his shirt and undershirt and discovered that the trocar hole, originally closed with a threaded plastic button, was belching liquid, probably propelled by a belly full of gas. His immense girth and the pressure of arms and hands had forced the liquids outward and onto his clothing. I replaced the trocar button, laid plastic sheeting against his bare belly, and sprayed Lysol around the casket. It sufficed until the visitation was over, and we were able to treat the problem later more thoroughly. I had not been the embalmer in this case; whoever was had obviously not treated the thoracic and abdominal organs.

Those who leave a larger body behind make a larger impression on us all.

CHAPTER FIVE

Maggots, wax, and the most important job

HOW DO YOU SNAG the instant attention of a young class of mortuary students—or anyone else, for that matter? Just mention decapitation. Amazingly enough, it's a far more common cause of death than people think, particularly in cases of industrial or auto accidents.

Back in the 1970s, my classmates and I listened attentively as our embalming instructor detailed the proper procedure for restoring a victim who had suffered the separation of head from body. He outlined for us the fine art of plunging a wooden mop handle, sharpened on both ends, down the spinal column and positioning the head back onto the shoulders by inserting the opposite end into the corresponding column section. The surrounding skin would then be sutured and the sutures waxed over.

In my more than thirty years as a licensed embalmer, I have used this technique only twice. Both victims, one male and one female, were passengers in an automobile that a fully loaded gravel truck had struck head-on. Apparently the leading edge of the car's interior windshield frame had sliced off the heads of both occupants. Also, because of the tremendous force of the truck, the injuries were not cleanly administered. Jagged steel and glass had slammed into soft flesh, nearly obliterating all facial features. The only way to distinguish which head belonged to which body, in fact, was the long hair with feminine barrettes still affixed. I situated the heads back onto the corresponding shoulders, but otherwise there was far too much damage to complete a satisfactory restoration.

FIXING THE BODY

"They sure do good work here" is a comment I have been hearing more and more since I opened my own funeral home in 2001. My wife, who also works with me, did not quite understand its meaning at first. She assumed that people were congratulating us on our dignified, compassionate manner and the care we provided to client families and our visiting public. But actually, *good work*, when we're talking about funerals, is the term used in my part of the country to describe how natural dead bodies look while reposing in their respective caskets—and that all starts with embalming.

Injecting a preservative chemical into the right femoral artery or right common carotid artery and opening the accompanying vein allows the blood to drain out of the body, thus allowing the chemical to react with and preserve or harden the surrounding tissues. Today, formaldehyde-based chemicals "fix," or firm and preserve, human tissue to such a state as to allow for preparation of the body and the funeral to take place.

Without such treatment, the unforgettable odor of decomposition would greet funeral guests. Even biblical scholars made note of putrefaction: "Jesus lay in the tomb for three days; surely He stinketh." Biblical accounts report that the dead Jesus was anointed with spices, no doubt to abate inevitable odors. And Shakespeare's scene in which Romeo visits Juliet in her family's mausoleum for one last kiss? No way. Since Juliet wasn't really dead yet, she would have smelled just fine. But her grandparents' remains would have knocked poor Romeo right out of his socks.

The Egyptians were the first true embalmers. The Egyptians removed the brain through the nostrils with a pointed tool and then inserted natron-soaked linens. They removed the abdominal organs and treated that area as well. Because those organs had a mystical value, they were stored in decorative jars with carved lids depicting certain animals. The body was then wrapped in linen sheets dipped in spices and natron, a preservative, and—voilà!—a mummy.

This crude embalming process was successful, but there was another quality of the Egyptian process that resulted in the mummies we see today. The arid Egyptian climate lacked humidity, which speeds decomposition. Without humidity, the body simply dries up if left outdoors, whether or not any preservation is attempted.

By the early 1800s, time was of the essence in preparing the deceased. The dead needed to be buried in a hurry to avoid the inevitable ravages of decomposition. And until the 1860s, undertakers could offer only ice to retard the inevitable decomposition process. But early undertakers realized that if surrounding meat with ice, straw, and even salt successfully kept it fresh for a few days, then might such a procedure work with human bodies too? Ice was a precious commodity back in the day, so a premium price was added to the undertaker's bill if a bereaved family desired to have their loved one viewed in the home or in the church. And so the first "cooling boards" were developed, crude wooden tables with a shallow metal pan to allow for ice to be placed under the deceased. Sometimes the deceased was viewed and eulogized while reposing on the cooling board, but on most occasions, the body was placed into a wood coffin after any ceremony and then buried. The cooling board was improved and refined over the years to include padding for the reposing deceased and hinges in the center for easier transport and storage. Cooling boards in the early 1900s were transported along with the embalmer's other necessary equipment to the deceased's home.

But then Dr. Thomas Holmes, a physician who had been fascinated with cadavers in college, experimented with fellow medical students to devise a preservative to allow the cadavers to last longer for more instruction time at school. Holmes tinkered with arsenic, mercury, and zinc compounds in solutions as possible preservatives, and arsenic seemed the best candidate.

During the Civil War, President Lincoln was greatly disappointed that many of the war dead from his hometown had to be buried on the battlefield because rapid decomposition precluded their transportation back home. Dr. Holmes offered his experimental arterial embalming procedure to the War Department in 1861. In a field hospital setting, Holmes and his assistants made an incision in any available area of the body. If the deceased had incurred trauma to the head and neck, then they made an incision into the femoral (upper thigh) space, raised the femoral artery and vein, and inserted an arsenic-based solution into the artery via a hand pump. In that way, by distributing the liquid throughout the arterial system, the blood would drain through the venous system. The arsenic solution replaced the blood, which was a major source of odor and decomposition, and "fixed" the tissues to retard or delay the ravages of decomposition.

The preservative qualities of the solution were amazing for the era, but there were serious problems associated with the arsenic. Because of its severe toxicity, the arsenic solution made several of Holmes's assistants ill and even proved fatal to a few battlefield embalmers. With no protective gloves available and a general lack of personal hygiene, arsenic on bare skin was hazardous. Danger notwithstanding, President Lincoln was reported to be summarily impressed with Holmes's efforts and commended him. Holmes was always trying new methods of preservation, including alcohol, but the advent of formaldehyde proved a watershed development.

Formaldehyde was cheap and safer than arsenic-based solutions, but best of all, it proved the best preservative ever conceived, the very one used almost exclusively today. After the Civil War, arterial embalming dwindled because of a lack of interest and the fact that so few were capable of performing the procedure. Dr. Holmes maintained his keen interest in embalming and began to develop, sell, and demonstrate his preservative fluid to undertakers around the country who would entertain the presentation. If Dr. Holmes had trained an undertaker, then the undertaker could refer to himself as an embalmer and could take advantage of the new preservation technique to garner new customers who were anxious for the opportunity to view their dead for a longer period of time and to actually schedule a funeral ceremony instead of hurriedly placing their loved one into the ground. In 1882, the Cincinnati College of Embalming (now the Cincinnati College of Mortuary Science) began operations with a precise emphasis on embalming.

Today the embalming process buys time—enough time to hold a funeral visitation and service three or four days after a death. Embalming, however, is not forever.

The procedure merely retards decomposition for a matter of days, or perhaps weeks. In time, the skin begins to leather and eventually assumes a grayish-brown tint, known among funeral directors as formaldehyde gray.

HE LOOKS JUST LIKE HIMSELF

Years ago I worked at a funeral home where comments concerning deceased appearances were universally negative. Rarely were congratulations expressed—much to the ongoing chagrin of my former employer. As the low man on the totem pole and an infrequent, inexperienced embalmer, my input was neither encouraged nor welcomed. But when the chief embalmer resigned, his duties fell to me, and a marked improvement began.

My older brother had always stressed that people come to a funeral home to see a deceased loved one looking natural and well groomed. The smallest details, from buffed fingernails and hand placement to an impeccable knot in a gentleman's necktie, are equally essential. That dedication to a dignified presentation has stuck with me to this day, and I have repeatedly stressed and ranted to my own sons that such devotion to duty is the only thing I will accept.

In time, my former boss, who no longer felt the need to enter the preparation room at all, was duly impressed and delighted with the sudden satisfaction of his clientele. In those archaic times, he would greet the deceased's family upon their arrival and then take full credit for the "good work," as if he had performed everything in the prepping stage.

My next stop on the employment road found me at a funeral home where the employees felt as I did—that the attractive appearance of the deceased, not the sale of an expensive casket, should be the ultimate goal. Although most funeral home visitors briefly admire the casket in which the decedent is reposing, as well as the spray of flowers adorning it and other bouquets blanketing the entire area, it can be difficult to distinguish one casket from another. The deceased loved one is the star. Rarely have I heard departing guests whisper, "Wow, Stan sure had a beautiful casket." More likely they say, "Wow, Stan looked like he could get up and talk to you; they sure do good work here."

That good work unfortunately seems to be missing from today's corporate-owned funeral homes. The company's stock exchange performance and the general manager's bonus expectations are far more important. One result is the purging of experienced embalmers and funeral directors in favor of kids fresh out of mortuary school who lack the proper seasoning but whose salary requirements meet bottom-line qualifications. As an elderly embalmer informed me many years ago, "It takes at least ten years to become a professional." I share that adage with my sons on a daily basis.

To present a dead human for viewing to his or her grieving family sounds like a strange custom. Why is it necessary that the deceased be present for a funeral to take place? Simple—it satisfies the need to say good-bye to a vessel that once held a beloved soul and that others still carry a strong emotional attachment toward.

In *The American Way of Death* (1963), the author Jessica Mitford heavily criticized the way that Americans care for our dead, particularly in regard to our purchases of ornate and costly caskets. Mitford also railed about the funeral ceremony itself and the display of a dead individual looking as if alive. Her scathing book gained a substantial following, and the ideas she proposed were moving quickly toward universal acceptance—until a sudden, tragic pivotal event occurred. President John F. Kennedy was assassinated mere months after her book's release.

BARBARIC—OR NATURAL?

With the death of President Kennedy, what did America see for the first time on live national television? A funeral of the grandest proportions, complete with a dead human contained in a very expensive solid mahogany casket, provided by a funeral home in Washington, D.C. That wasn't the casket from Texas, however. Upon Kennedy's death on November 22, the Secret Service contacted a Dallas funeral home to come to Parkland Memorial Hospital with the finest casket available. The dutiful director arrived with a solid bronze casket into which Kennedy's unembalmed body was placed. The president was then spirited off to the airport and flown to Andrews Air Force Base for an autopsy by navy doctors.

It was later reported that an actual tug-of-war with President Kennedy's body occurred between Secret Service agents and the Dallas county sheriff. The sheriff correctly noted that a homicide victim should be autopsied in the county of death, but he was overruled, and the body left Dallas. The temporary casket was never paid for, although the Dallas funeral director billed the Kennedy family on numerous occasions. After never receiving payment, he mentioned the problem to a newspaper reporter, and the negative publicity from the story damaged his image so much that his business suffered and eventually closed. The same bronze casket was stored in the basement of the White House for several years until 1967, when Robert F. Kennedy, the president's brother, had it unceremoniously dropped into the Atlantic Ocean.

Secret Service agents accompanied Kennedy's body throughout its travels, from the trip back to Washington, D.C., to the naval hospital's autopsy room, and finally to the funeral home. One agent, unimpressed with the pomp and circumstance of the funeral and believing the embalming process was a crude, barbaric, and unnecessary procedure, wondered why Kennedy wasn't just cremated, since there was so much damage to his head. Later, however, that same agent was reported to have been totally amazed at the work of the embalmers and their restoration process. He had watched as the formaldehyde-based chemical was injected and the color quickly came back to the president's face. The Kennedy family was able to privately view the body in a most presentable state, looking very natural—unlike what Mrs. Kennedy had experienced in Dallas, when she was photographed attempting to retrieve pieces of her husband's skull and brain tissue from the trunk lid of their open limousine.

SUPERGLUE AND SKELETONS

So, is it really a good thing to embalm and restore a body, then put cosmetics on it and dress it in its Sunday best to display as if the person were still alive? Ironically, in nearly every case of someone who dies over the age of seventy-five, the family is very satisfied with the appearance of the deceased.

A young person, however, presents the ultimate grief experience to his or her family, which is often compounded by a need for extensive restoration, since young people tend to die tragically. A face that has been bludgeoned, smashed, traumatized, burned, lacerated, or exposed to the ravages of cancer presents a challenge too, regardless of how sharp the funeral director's skills may be. There is no greater sense of helplessness than needing to tell a mother and father that their son or daughter cannot be viewed because of too much disease or damage, not enough body parts, too many days in the July sun, or too many weeks of lying in a river.

Summer heat results in a body that turns on itself. Stomach acids and gases erode and destroy the body from the inside out. Once maggots develop, the body can be reduced to a skeleton in a matter of days. Too much time submerged in deep water creates similar decomposition problems, with a greater incidence of bloating and discoloration, which often results in a closed casket.

If any semblance of the person's face is present, however, then restoration can take place. Time-tested methods can repair even blunt-force trauma from an auto accident. Lacerations are secured with superglue, rather than sewn, which leaves a raised trail from the thread. Broken facial bones are pushed back into place and wired together. Large holes from rearview mirrors, radio knobs, gearshift levers, turn-signal stalks, and windshield glass can be filled with wax and reshaped like the former contours of the face. Lips, orbital bones, and even eyeballs can be fashioned from wax. Eyebrows, eyelashes, and facial hair can be harvested from the back of the deceased's head and then inserted into soft wax in the appropriate areas.

However, a body run over by a train, caught in an explosion, hit by a shotgun blast, killed in a plane crash, or burned in a fire is generally a hopeless case. Burned beyond recognition is a lost cause; there is only a black skeleton to work with. I have attempted a facial reconstruction in such a situation, and with poor results. Working from a photo, I have constructed a face and all its features from wax; filled clothing with cotton to simulate chest, arms, and abdomen; and even attached white gloves to the cuffs of a blouse so that hands appeared present—not a very natural appearance, but close enough for the family to derive some sort of closure from a devastating loss.

Once I discovered the utility of plaster of Paris, restoring large defects of the head became simpler. A young man I cared for recently had been attempting to discover the object that was obstructing the travel of a large hydraulic press at an automotive parts production facility. He placed his head inside the press, and unfortunately, the press engaged and flattened his head to the shape of a pancake.

After embalming the lower portion of the body, I set out to repair his head. The press had caused massive scalp and facial tears, so I knew there would be a great deal of superglue involved. I used my gloved hand to push wet plaster of Paris into the area that was once his mouth, and amazingly enough, the plaster expanded as it dried. I continued to push the material into the defect until it completely popped his features back into an almost-normal position. I was then able to glue the multiple lacerations and apply cosmetics to eventually achieve a very natural appearance.

MAGGOTS AND THE MAGIC OF LIME

During summer months, there are increased cases not only of rapid decomposition as a result of drownings but also of people who happen to die alone at home and are not discovered for several days. With severe decomposition, the skin slips off the body, bloating occurs, and the tremendously offensive odor does not allow for normal viewing. In years past, a formaldehyde-based chemical was poured over the body to mask the odor, but even that could not completely eliminate the smell.

A funeral director employer of mine from many years ago introduced me to the positive effects of agricultural lime. Lime is the white drying agent familiar to those who watch Mafia-themed movies, where hit men bury dispatched victims in shallow graves and then cover the bodies with a hundred pounds of lime. Because lime rapidly absorbs any liquids, in the case of a decomposing human body, it eliminates those odiferous liquids; thus, the body is less likely to be discovered. In this day and age, however, skeletal remains can still be identified.

As a farmer, this man had poured lime into the graves of dead livestock and rightly assumed that the same treatment would suffice for humans. Before the deceased is placed in a normal casket or cremation container, a bed of lime eight inches deep is poured into the casket. The deceased is then placed on top of the initial bed of lime, and then completely covered with additional lime. This process requires two fifty-pound bags, which eliminate the odor within minutes. I have also used lime with wonderful results on decubitus ulcers (bedsores) and other odor problems. Other funeral directors in my area have called to inquire about how to handle agricultural lime in a funeral home setting.

Many years ago, I embalmed the body of a twenty-two-year-old man who had been hit by a passing freight train. Luckily, he was killed instantaneously on impact. But the engine did not pass over his body; he was flung alongside the tracks. Since this occurred back in the 1970s, long before the days of obligatory lawsuits, an autopsy was not performed. The county coroner correctly determined at the scene that this was an accidental death.

But since this man carried no identification, I embalmed the body and held it. Three weeks went by, with several visits from grieving parents of missing sons, all deeply torn. Their pain was excruciating to watch. Might we now bury our long-lost boy and perhaps derive some sort of closure? Or do we pray that this body is not really his?

Although facial features were still clearly recognizable, formaldehyde gray was making its presence known. I had liberally applied a massage cream to retain tissue pliability, and I soon decided to add paste cosmetics to mask the impending changes.

Identification finally came five weeks later. A trembling father had seen flyers published in his local newspaper. His son had stormed out after a disagreement over farm chores. He was ultimately identified by his unique work boots—and a missing ring finger from an earlier tractor accident on his dad's property.

Another time, I removed the body of a young man from underneath a school bus he had been repairing. The jacks supporting the bus had failed, and the rear dual wheels crushed him. Unfortunately, he was working alone during the noon hour when other mechanics had left for lunch. When his coworkers returned, they made a horrific discovery. The man had been underneath the bus for at least an hour, and another hour or so had passed before my arrival—ample time for nature's effects, such as the gathering of flies. I brought him back to the funeral home to begin the embalming process and noticed some tiny fly larvae in the corner of his mouth and the corner of one eye. I brushed them aside and thought nothing more of it.

After meeting with the young man's mother the next day to make the funeral arrangements, she requested that she view her son immediately, even before he was dressed and placed in his casket. I asked her to join me back at the funeral home in two hours. Thank goodness I granted myself the extra time.

When I went into the preparation room, I was aghast. When I looked at the man's face, it appeared to be moving. With a pair of tweezers I pulled open his mouth and found it full of slimy, squirming maggots. I dipped cotton into liquid formaldehyde and pushed it inside, but it had little effect on those rascals, and being a novice in the funeral business at that time, I was at a loss as to my next move. I called my more experienced older brother. He sagely informed me that, since maggots have a slimy coating, only kerosene would cut through it to kill them. So that's what I used.

ORGAN DONATION AND EMBALMING

Time can be an issue when organ donation is a factor. Tissue banks from around the country are becoming more aggressive in their quests to acquire hearts, lungs, kidneys, skin, eyes, ears, bones, and other harvestable human body parts. Many hospitals' death-reporting forms even include spaces for families to check whether they wish the tissue retrieval organization to be contacted.

I happen to be a big fan of organ donation. An unbelievable amount of good has come from it, and we all might need a new part or two someday. Young people involved in accidents who are brain dead are ideal candidates for donating their organs. Their bodies are kept alive for transplantation once family members say good-bye and grant their permission. I am quite surprised, however, that even elderly bones are in demand. Apparently, they can be crushed into a fine powdery mix and used in knee-replacement surgery.

My only problem with tissue donation is the lack of expediency. Educating the public and making funeral directors and families keenly aware of the Tissue Bank's valuable service is all well and good, but when the time comes to actually remove the needed tissue, it takes too long. I have had to wait more than a day on several occasions before I could retrieve a body to start the funeral process, and embalming is more difficult after the body has been kept in a hospital cooler for several hours.

THE TOUGHEST RESTORATIONS

Suicides present their own unique restorative challenges. My first experience came as a wide-eyed fifteen-year-old. My brother and I were dispatched to a residence to remove the victim of a self-inflicted shotgun blast to the face. That was considered in its day a simple, open-and-shut case. The coroner had already come and gone and granted permission for the deceased to be removed. The man's daughter greeted us at the front door and showed us into a small first-floor bathroom with just a commode, a sink, and a ceiling coated with fragments of human tissue.

The man had placed the shotgun in his mouth as he sat on the toilet seat. His head was nearly gone; the blast had blown away all structures from the upper lip and above. Brain and skull pieces with hair still attached adorned the ceiling and hung downward like stalactites. Only the lower jaw still rested on the decedent's neck. I was so stunned that I barely remember the removal procedure. Did we carry in the litter or just roll up the cot to the bathroom door? Who knows?

The daughter followed us outside to the hearse and asked whether part of our job was to scrub down the bathroom. My brother said no. However, when the woman said she would pay someone "a handsome sum" to do so, I readily spoke up. But my brother nixed the deal, saying that if I did a poor job, her family might not ever call our establishment again. Just as well, since I don't know how I would have tackled that mess—although my fifteen-year-old mind kept spinning endlessly in regard to what "a handsome sum" might be.

Some restorations require many hours of effort, but others are much simpler. Many embalmers routinely fill women's brassieres with cotton for the appearance of full, lifelike breasts. But the proper quantity sometimes involves a bit of guesswork. One grieving husband confronted me upon first viewing his late wife in her casket, inquiring as to how I had magically increased her bust size. At first I was apprehensive, thinking he might be angry with me—but then he winked and told me his wife would be proud to be sporting such an exquisite pair.

CHAPTER SIX

I wonder why you called us…

IF SOMEONE DOES NOT volunteer it to me immediately, I ask why he or she came to us for service. It's been said that the best form of advertising is word of mouth, which I can attest is true. I have conducted a huge number of funeral services for families that have called on me because of a recommendation from another family that I served in the past. The old adage "funerals begat funerals" is another time-tested fact that is applicable to the business today. Many times over the years I have heard the comment, "Our family came to your funeral home because we were just here last month for John Doe's funeral and everything was so nicely done."

I use the tried-and-true advertising techniques, most important, billboards and television. A marketing specialist informed me several years ago that a funeral home such as my family operation would achieve great results with outdoor billboards with our family photo incorporated on each one. Educate the public that our family will personally care for their family in their time of need.

I have six billboards strategically placed in my service area so they are seen on the most heavily traveled roads. My wife insists that we change the text of the printed message and, of course, our outfits. Every six months we arrange for a family photo shoot for our new billboard picture. I know it works because people call to acknowledge that they have seen the new billboard. We caused a stir of congratulatory phone calls recently when my daughter-in-law and our first grandson were included in the latest billboard picture. All of us pictured, my wife, daughter, two sons, and daughter-in-law, received positive comments from our friends, and even strangers—"Hey, I saw you on a billboard the other day." Folks stop me in banks, gas stations, restaurants, and other places in town to acknowledge seeing my image on the billboards. Billboards are golden for us, and they prove to me that newspaper and telephone book advertisements have a lesser impact.

My marketing specialist lady also enlightened me about television advertising. At first I was hesitant because of the tremendous cost, but as she emphasized, "It takes money to make money." She suggested that I stand in front of the camera and personally deliver my commercial message as opposed to a voice-over with photos and facts flashing across the screen. She informed me that if I were to use merely a voice-over and no live-action speaking, then I might as well do a radio advertisement. I have done a few radio commercial spots over the years, but there is no doubt that television ads have a much better impact and response from potential customers. I can't tell you how many folks called me or stopped me on the street to tell me how impressed they were with the television commercial. I even got a big head at a visitation one evening when I happened to overhear an older man whisper to his wife, "Look, there's *the* Mr. Webster; I saw him on TV yesterday."

I must admit that I am pleasantly surprised that even today, less costly advertising and promotional items have garnered calls for service for me. My sons and I go through two boxes of business cards each a year, handing them out during visitations and funerals, and especially out in public. Our family photo adorns each business card, a stellar idea that real estate agents made popular years ago. I was playing golf early one morning a few years ago and was approached by the course manager, who said I looked familiar to him. I introduced myself and handed him a couple of my business cards. He said he knew my oldest sister and then thanked me for the cards. He jokingly asked me whether I thought he looked like he needed a funeral director. Two months later, the same gentleman called on me to take care of his son, who had unexpectedly died, and when his wife passed away a year later, I handled her funeral arrangements as well.

A bereaved family came to the funeral home one evening and requested that we take care of their late mother. The son of the deceased produced one of my business cards and stated that a kindly minister had handed the card to him at the hospital's intensive-care-unit waiting room just that afternoon. The son explained that his mother's doctor was in the process of detailing to the family that all hope for his mother's recovery was lost and that she would surely expire in the next few hours. As the family exploded in grief at the news, the son said that a minister who was tending to another family in the waiting area approached his family and began to pray with them. The son thanked the unknown clergyman for his act of unexpected kindness and compassion and stated that his family had no clue where to turn next. The minister reached for his wallet and presented the son with my business card and told him, "Go see Mr. Webster; he will be glad to assist you and I know him well." The son could not recall the minister's name, and I still to this day do not know who that particular pastor might have been.

Another surprisingly effective promotional item is the fancy ink pens that I present to folks in mass quantities. Again, on the advice of my marketing friend, I now purchase expensive ballpoint pens (with my name and phone number on them, of course) and offer them to people just as I would a business card. If people ask to borrow my pen, I hand it over and tell them to keep it. My pens are thick with a padded grip, trimmed in gold and cost more than

$3 each. If you offer people a cheap pen, then they have a cheap pen; offer them a quality, expensive pen and they are impressed that it is theirs to keep and are not likely to forget who presented it to them. My sons and I have a pocketful of pens with us at all times and make sure we hand them out every day, if possible. When we go to remove a deceased loved one from a hospital, a nursing care facility, or even a private residence, anyone present or nearby receives an official Webster Funeral Home pen. The nurses and caregivers at the local hospice unit greet us when we arrive with a familiar refrain: "We need some more of your nice pens."

A family called recently and requested that we come to the residence to remove their late mother. The caller on the line stated that he was calling our funeral home because his next-door neighbor always had one of my pens in his pocket and often told folks in the neighborhood that I had once given him a handful of pens one day.

Whenever I go to deliver a prearrangement presentation in a group setting, I always leave two pens at each attendee's seat. Many times attendees approach me at the conclusion of the presentation to return the pens but are happy when they realize the pens are theirs to keep.

Speaking engagements are the ultimate seed planters. When I started in the funeral business many years ago, I worked for an employer who despised public speaking, and if a group requested a presentation from the funeral home, I was instructed to be the sacrificial lamb. My employer would tell me that such public presentations were a waste of time and that those in attendance consistently asked the most idiotic questions. I, however, welcomed the opportunity not only to gain some possible customers but also to educate a public yearning to know about what goes on in a funeral home, and especially how much it is going to cost. My former employer probably won't admit it, but there were many funerals at that funeral home because of my "pre-need" presentations. (When we are called for service upon the death of a loved one, that is considered "at-need." When someone who is very much alive decides to arrange and pay for their funeral services before their own death, that is "pre-need.")

Since I opened my funeral home in 2001, I have actively offered to speak to Veterans of Foreign Wars groups, retirement communities, and churches. Nearly every request I have made is positively acknowledged, and most every time an appointment is made for such a speaking engagement. For the first few seminars I conducted, I came prepared with a briefcase stuffed full of insurance applications, contracts, and ink pens, assuming I would be inundated with a new crop of customers. Alas, such is not the case. I have not once completed a sale at the conclusion of one of my seminars—most likely because folks are hesitant to attempt to complete such documentation in such a public forum, and I completely understand. Perhaps folks are concerned that their peers might overhear some of their answers to required questions, especially when a monetary amount is discussed.

However, just like billboard advertising, television advertising, ink pens, or business cards, a personal appearance seminar is a sure-fire seed planter. Even the informational brochures I hand out plant the seed in the potential customer's mind to remember my funeral home when the need arises. I have had so many customers come to me to prearrange their funeral services because they attended one of my seminars two or three years earlier. A gentleman called recently to inform me of his wife's death. During our initial conversation, he thanked me for being so informative when he and his late wife attended a pre-need presentation I had delivered three years prior at a Ford Motor Company retirees' luncheon.

There are cases where funeral directors have woven their own networking webs by mingling at various civic functions, especially anything church related. Bingo nights at churches have long been golden opportunities for directors to press the flesh, hand out draft beer and Cokes, and always be certain to pause and fawn over the elderly ladies—who are the mouthpieces of their church. They quickly spread the word when they find a funeral director whom they consider nice.

One longtime director friend who has since died was once considered the area's king of the church supper. He hit as many as possible on any given evening, and upon his departure, he would find the minister, thank him for his hospitality, and slip a crisp $50 bill into his palm—a huge sum in the 1940s. Which director do you suppose that minister recommended whenever a death in the church family occurred?

My elderly friend scored big in the 1950s with an ingenious promotional item, again targeting churchgoers. A traveling salesman was peddling high-priced grandfather-clock kits. He also had thirty large schoolhouse clocks stored in a warehouse, collecting dust, which he wished to dispose of. My friend proposed that if his funeral home's name were painted on the clocks' white faces, he would buy all thirty. Soon thirty local churches had new clocks positioned in their sanctuaries so that the clergy could see them clearly. Instead of glancing at their watches to be sure their sermons ended by noon, they glanced at the clocks—and at the same time etched the funeral home's name in their minds.

CHAPTER SEVEN

She is survived by...

JUST WHAT IS A wake, anyway? What about a visitation? A viewing? A memorial service? Clarification is sometimes necessary when detailing funeral events.

A visitation, sometimes still referred to as a wake, which long ago meant staying awake to spend time with the deceased and his or her family, still involves the act of spending time. A visitation means that people visit and pay respects to the deceased and his or her surviving family members. Friends and associates of the deceased's family come to the funeral home, sign the guest book, view the reposing deceased, and offer condolences to the family. Generally, most mourners leave after these obligatory acts, but other mourners will stay and have coffee, or just sit in the chapel for the entire visitation period. Also acceptable is *viewing,* which literally means to view the deceased.

The traditional wake, staying up with the deceased, is still sometimes practiced today. In my area there are many Southern Pentecostal families, for whom all-night visitations are quite common. Two or three times each year we conduct them, usually at churches. We deliver the deceased by four o'clock, and the visitation continues until the funeral service takes place the following day. It's noted in an obituary as follows: "Visitation after five o'clock Tuesday at the Church of Holy Grace until the time of the funeral service on Wednesday at eleven o'clock."

Different religions have different rites. Sometimes referred to as "sitting shiva," shiva is a Jewish burial rite consisting of friends visiting the home of a grieving family to offer condolences.

A funeral service or funeral ceremony is just what it says—a period of ritualistic actions, usually coordinated by a leader, to pay homage to one who has died, with his or her body present. A memorial service, or simply memorial, is much the same as a funeral service, only the body is not on-site. A memorial service is commonly conducted after someone has been cremated, as there is obviously no body to view.

Perhaps my thoughts on this subject are much ado about nothing, but I think that I should describe the services I perform daily with the utmost correctness, if for no other reason than respect. Funeral and burial rites can be conducted only one time for each person. If I attend to something improperly, I can't exactly ask for a do-over.

THE OBIT

I have noticed that newspaper writers enjoy taking poetic license by referring to a *casket* in one paragraph and then a *coffin* in the next (see chapter 10 to find out which one is correct). Also, obituary writers in many newspapers merely enter detailed information that the funeral homes dictate to them. Since there is a per-line charge, the family can submit whatever information they want.

But it's when a feature writer writes an obituary for a celebrity or high-profile death that problems begin. Rarely do those obituaries end properly. They include such technical errors as saying that "funeral *services*" will be held or "memorial *services*" will take place at such-and-such a day and time. Well, there is only one funeral or memorial service. In a Catholic obituary, we would never say, "Masses of Christian Burial will be held…" In a Jewish obituary, we would never say, "Shivas to be observed at…"

My personal pet peeve, however, is when obits list the order of events in reverse, with the funeral service mentioned first and only then the visitation hours. Chronological order is far easier for readers to follow. Newspaper writers also commit errors that to me are unforgivable, such as misspelling *cemetery* as *cemetary* or using *internment* instead of *interment*, which have very different meanings!

Funeral directors can sometimes be blamed for poor obituary writing; the director making the arrangements compiles and writes most of them. One common grammatical blunder is referring to certain relatives as brother-in-laws as opposed to brothers-in-law. But even well-meaning family members who try to assist in the compilation of obituary information are guilty of embarrassing snafus. A few people intentionally omit certain irritant brothers, sisters, or cousins. But others unwittingly hurt the feelings of grandchildren or siblings by referring to only one of them as "Mom's favorite grandchild, Freddy," or by saying, "survived by three sons, especially her special caregiver, Tom."

Family members can cause all sorts of divisive issues.

ALL IN THE FAMILY

When an individual dies at home, generally there is a houseful of people gathered at the bedside. This is a scene that a funeral director has to carefully observe and take in, because important conclusions can be drawn from it. Those present usually exhibit genuine sorrow. However, it is sometimes possible to detect that those sobbing at Grandma's bedside are only upset that their gravy train has been derailed and they can't borrow any more money from her.

When the family is assembled, they often tell me which day and time they want the visitation and funeral to take place. We note such information and save them from having to endure more questions later at the funeral arrangement conference.

When it comes time to leave the family's residence with their deceased loved one in tow, it can be emotionally wrenching. I have received numerous requests not to cover the deceased's face. Grown sons have assisted us in carrying the cot. Family members have run down the street after the hearse as we slowly pull away.

After the body has been removed from the place of death, we set up a time for the bereaved family to come in for the arrangement conference. The funeral arrangement conference is when the funeral director sits down with the member or members of the deceased's family to acquire the necessary information to complete the death certificate, compile information for the obituary, arrange for the service selections, be it ground burial or cremation, and allow the family to select any merchandise they desire, whether it is a casket and burial vault or a cremation urn.

Even as a funeral director of many years, I still, on occasion, get that feeling of butterflies in my stomach or a slight feeling of trepidation when the bereaved family approaches the front door of the funeral home for the first time.

We look for all kinds of signs as to what might happen. A bereaved family who has been asked to arrive at ten o'clock in the morning and happens to be late is sometimes thought of as a bad omen. A former employer of mine used to swear that when a family is late for their appointment to make arrangements, then it is more likely that the family will not pay the bill or that there will be trouble in collecting the bill. His thought was that if a family is late showing up then they must be irresponsible.

The initial viewing of a deceased loved one is another time of potential butterflies for the funeral director. Even if you are extremely confident that the deceased looks very natural, there is still a small degree of doubt that speaks to you: "I hope the family is pleased; what if they are not?" We all want that gushing exclamation by the assembled family—"He looks great" or "Mom looks absolutely beautiful; you have done a wonderful job"—as a resounding seal of approval.

I sometimes feel a wee bit slighted if a family does not immediately express sheer delight at their loved one's appearance. Some situations reveal a delayed seal of approval. I give the family several minutes alone for their initial viewing before I go to them at the casket to make sure they are satisfied. On that walk up to the casket, as brief as it is, there are many thoughts running through my head: Are the lips too pink or not pink enough? Is the hair styled properly? Is the necktie straight? Is her dress smoothed out just right? My wife checks the work of my sons and I with a fine-toothed comb once the deceased is placed into the casket, and again when the casket is placed into the chapel, and again just before the family arrives. Yet even with all that redundancy there is still the worry that something might need to be addressed—after all, someone's loved one is lying in repose, so everything must be right.

The desired seal-of-approval moment sometimes comes when the family is departing the funeral home at the conclusion of the visitation period. Parting compliments include "Mom looked beautiful, and we can't thank you enough," or the tearful proclamation, "Everything was perfect." Such positive feedback is the hope and expectation of every funeral director worth his salt.

Who's Really the Next of Kin?

Sometimes there are family problems, however, that exist in the family itself. My son and I once pulled the hearse into the driveway of a mansion, exited the vehicle, and made our way to the front porch. The elderly gentleman, whom I recalled as a recent pre-need customer, had passed and was found in his bedroom suite on the second floor, surrounded by several grieving family members.

One of the deceased man's daughters introduced herself to me and took me by the arm, directing me to a vacant bedroom down the hall. She said that I should speak to her and her alone concerning her late father's funeral arrangements. She further stated that there were some current grumblings in the family and that she would be in my office as soon as possible. We removed her father from his residence, loaded him into the hearse, and soon noticed that the daughter was following close behind us for the trip back to the funeral home. Since it was after 11 p.m., I found her actions to be a little out of the ordinary. We unloaded the deceased and, as my son rolled him into the preparation room, I proceeded to light up the interior of the building and unlock the front door.

The daughter of the deceased rushed in and quickly informed me that her late father's housekeeper had just recently become his wife. The daughter was concerned as to who was to be responsible for the funeral expenses. Luckily, the elderly gentleman had prearranged and prepaid for his funeral services with me just months before his death; otherwise, this arrangement conference would have been a nightmare. I seated the daughter and excused myself to retrieve her father's pre-arrangement file. I showed her that her father and I had sat down just recently and finalized his funeral arrangements and that he had prepaid. This pleased the daughter, yet she was very concerned about her late father's property and other valuable belongings.

She went on to weave a tale to me that she and her late father had been estranged for many years, and that in a period of extreme loneliness, her father had agreed to the prodding of his young, live-in housekeeper of just a few months and had married her. The daughter had recently discovered that her father had decided to leave all of his worldly goods and possessions to his new bride, and his children were to gain not a thing. I felt sorry for her and her situation but explained that her late father's wife was the legal next of kin and the number-one decision maker.

The next morning the new widow in question arrived at my office alone and proceeded to verify all the information and selections her late husband had arranged for, including shipping his body back to his native East Coast for burial. The spouse was keenly aware of the fact that her late husband's children harbored a profound hatred toward her. She wanted a private funeral ceremony with only her and the casketed remains of her husband present. She said she was willing to allow her late husband's children to have a public viewing and funeral the next day, without her presence.

So that is exactly what occurred—the first funeral for the wife was the only time I had ever conducted a service with only the deceased, the officiating minister, and one mourner. The second service the next day was well attended by his family and many mourners, and officiated by the same minister.

Second marriages can make for some strange proceedings. A gruff woman of seventy years sat with me to arrange for her late husband's funeral services. Before I could begin my normal arrangement conference procedure, she quickly interrupted me with many questions: Was a newspaper obituary required by law? Do stepchildren have any claim to a dead body? Could she have him cremated without his children's knowledge?

I explained to her that she, as the surviving spouse, had the right to arrange for the final disposition of her late husband's body. Morally, I mentioned to her, perhaps her late husband's children should be notified of the death-care plans. She replied that she had no plan to inform her husband's children of the death—those children despised her and rarely visited their father. She further stated that her late spouse's children would telephone only when they needed money or to be bailed out of jail. She asked me to present her with a proposal for direct cremation with no public viewing and no funeral ceremony.

When I asked the wife if she wanted to view her late husband before he was cremated, she replied, "I already saw him in the hospital before you got there to pick him up." We finalized the proposal and she left, only to come back a few hours later to inform me that she had changed her mind. She now wanted me to embalm, dress, and place her husband into a fiber-board casket so that she and her neighbor friend could privately view him before he was cremated.

When I informed the woman that I would charge for the extra requested services, she was very unhappy, referred to me as a rotten S.O.B., and accused me of overcharging her. She angrily left and called me the next morning to tell me that she would still like to see her late husband. I offered to dress him and place him in a rental cremation casket at no additional charge, to which she replied, "There better not be any charge for that." I sighed and told her to come over in a few hours for her private, no-extra-charge viewing.

In the meantime, the late gentleman's natural children received wind of their father's death and were calling to see about the time for the funeral. When I explained to the children that there was to be no funeral, they went ballistic and rained profanities on me the likes of which I had never heard.

I telephoned the spouse of the deceased and told her of my recent telephone encounters with her stepchildren. She laughed it off and told me that the reason she was having her late husband immediately cremated was so that his children would not have an opportunity to see him one last time. She justified her stance on the matter by declaring, "They would not come to see him when he was healthy, and they would not come see him when he was ill and infirm, so they are not going to see him when he's dead." That's a pretty strong sentiment on her part, although the strange part was yet to come.

After the cremation had taken place, I delivered the cremated remains of her late husband to her home. As I was walking away, she yelled for me to come back so she could ask a question. She asked about the toxicity of human cremated remains. I replied that, since the cremation process involves such tremendous heat, I was sure that the ashes were not toxic. She seemed happy with that answer and began to share with me that she and her late husband enjoyed taking a bath together in years past and she was planning on drawing a nice hot bath that evening and wanted to include sprinkling a few handfuls of her late husband's ashes into the steaming bathwater with her.

In this strange situation, I did what I could to ease the pain. No matter what the circumstances, during every stage of the funeral process, so much pain can be avoided. All you need is the trusted guidance of a director who displays professionalism and integrity, and who is willing to take the time to find out what you really want and need, what you can afford, and what you feel is appropriate.

WHO'S THE HOOKER WITH THE MINISTER?

The clergy can also make the situation better—or worse. Funeral directors and the clergy, through regular, ongoing contact, enjoy a close-knit relationship. They are often good friends, golfing partners, and sometimes even drinking buddies.

Priests and ministers can make or break a funeral home's reputation. In my first year in the business, I worked for a man who lavishly bestowed gifts on the clergy. When a minister first arrived at the funeral home to conduct a service, my boss would hand him a Cross pen-and-pencil set. The next time the pastor would receive Cincinnati Reds tickets; other times a crisp $100 bill would be pressed into his hand. "These people help us to stay in business," he would tell me. "Go out of your way to treat them well."

For Christmas, he would order expensive fruit baskets from a local florist, and we would deliver them personally to area ministers' homes. After about three years, my boss decided to curtail the practice, and you would not believe the fallout. Not only ministers but also their wives began calling us around December 20, wondering when their fruit would be delivered. When informed that we had cut back on gifting, they called us a bunch of cheapskates. We reinstituted the practice the following Christmas.

A few ministers can be real thorns in our sides. The senior pastor of one large Baptist congregation was not fond of my former boss. The good reverend of sixty years was married to a parishioner thirty years his junior—a woman notorious for her fine jewelry and tight-fitting clothing—much to the embarrassment of the congregation. The first time my former employer caught sight of the couple was when the reverend came to the funeral home to attend a visitation. My boss asked in a loud voice, "Who's the hooker with the minister?"

Over the next few months of obituary reading, we couldn't help but notice that other funeral homes were servicing deceased members of that congregation. When I was finally able to arrange a funeral with the minister, I asked on our way to the cemetery why he had been avoiding us. He proceeded to rail on and on about my boss and finally admitted that he'd encouraged his congregation never to enter our establishment again.

Years ago, Catholic parishes were small neighborhoods of only a few streets, and parish members exclusively patronized the local funeral home. These days, with folks moving to suburbs and declining enrollments, that relationship has also slowed. Also, Catholic dioceses in some cities have begun building funeral homes on Catholic cemetery property and then goading parishioners into using those homes: "The local diocese would appreciate it if you would consider the funeral home on our cemetery grounds when the need arises." The church's use of its tax-exempt status to construct a for-profit funeral home will probably be the last straw in straining our relations.

Many years ago, I held several funerals at a fundamentalist church, where the minister promoted himself and his facility at every opportunity. "If Mr. Jones could rise up out of that casket and talk to you right now," he'd bellow, "he would tell you to come here every Sunday morning, every Sunday evening, every Wednesday evening, and every Saturday evening. If you want to hear the true word of God, then you must come here!"

At one particularly rousing service, he came down from the pulpit and brought the whole front row of family members to tears—of anger. The deceased was a forty-five-year-old father who'd left a wife and twin sixteen-year-old daughters. Both girls were high school cheerleaders. The minister pointed his finger directly at them and shouted, "If your daddy could rise from death today, he would tell you two to stop displaying your bodies in wicked ways with those little cheerleader outfits." Although most of the congregation voiced agreement with hearty rejoinders of "Amen, brother," the family was not pleased.

That minister was known to "tell it like it is." He once declared to those assembled at a funeral service that the deceased, a divorced man and known drinker, was no doubt "in a devil's hell, in a lake of fire, with not a drop of water to cool his tongue." Once again, attending family members were not happy.

The minister's congregation was not shy about sharing their beliefs, either. As I was manning the front door at a visitation one evening, a member of his congregation asked me where I went to church. When I responded, she said, "Well, I really feel sorry for you, because you are surely going to hell." When I asked why, she responded that only her church members would ever get to heaven.

CHAPTER EIGHT

I need to be up front—I was his favorite cousin!

BEHAVIOR IN GENERAL, ALONG with styles of dress at funerals, has reached new lows. I suppose this is reflected in other aspects of modern life as well—even churches encourage folks to come as they are, and airline travelers no longer don their Sunday best, not even in first class. So teenagers attend funerals wearing rock-band-emblazoned T-shirts, cutoff shorts, and sandals. Girls float in wearing hip-hugger pants that expose not only their bellies but also the cracks of their buttocks.

Adults may dress a bit better, but their actions leave much to be desired. Some who attend visitations stand right outside the funeral home door, venturing inside for only a moment to sign the guest book and make their presences known—but otherwise they puff on cigarettes, spit tobacco juice, and spew raw profanity accompanied by plenty of raucous laughter. Not exactly a pleasant experience for more respectful mourners who hold their breath as they walk through acrid clouds of smoke, dodge puddles of brown phlegm, and close their ears to offensive language.

Rude smokers continually astonish me by flipping cigarette butts into our decorative mulch and onto our pavement or by stubbing them out in our concrete entryway. I've even seen people emptying their overflowing car ashtrays into the funeral home's parking lot.

Children at funeral homes are always a sticky subject, depending on their ages and maturity levels. We funeral directors don't appreciate being drafted as baby-sitters, but unfortunately, such is often the case. Four-year-old Jimmy and three-year-old Janie have no business being allowed to roam free and unmonitored in a place filled with distraught, weeping grownups—and untold opportunities for getting into mischief.

I have seen small children knock over flower vases; push over lamps; yank every tissue out of a box and then toss all of them onto the floor; pull pictures off walls and onto themselves; jump off chairs and couches; remove couch cushions and hurl them onto the carpet; repeatedly kick walls with their new leather shoes; pitch entire rolls of toilet paper into commodes; turn restroom water faucets on and leave them on; slam doors over and over; and rub their dirty fingerprints on walls, molding, and door glass. What gets me most is any parent who thinks it is so cute when Junior holds the front door open for visitors, thereby letting out the air-conditioning and letting in flies and other insects.

Parents, occupied with greeting visitors, can easily fail to keep track of their brood. But I have heard a few declare that they expect my staff (and me!) to watch their children while they speak to relatives. One informed me that I needed to build a playground on the property to keep her children occupied.

I am all for allowing little ones to view and say good-bye to deceased loved ones, but if they are unlikely to remain at their parents' sides or in the custody of an older sibling, then they should be left at home.

I WAS ONLY TRYING TO HELP!

The elderly funeral director for whom I worked in the 1970s told me that you could always tell the class of people at a visitation by the number standing outside smoking—or by the number who strolled in carrying bottles of soda pop. I provide coffee and soft drinks at no charge, but at least once a month I kick myself over it. When something is free, people often have no regard for the amount they consume. I expect some lack of discretion among children, but I actually have more problems with adults. Grown men and women will exit a funeral home with three or four cans of soda tucked under their arms for the ride home.

After questioning a lady about this once, she said she was taking a can home to her mother who couldn't make it to the visitation. And after watching two overweight little boys consume six pops apiece in one evening, I told them that they'd had enough. Their mother overheard and cursed at me for denying her sons the pleasure of a seventh soda. I hark back to the wisdom of my 1970s employer: he said that the mark of a classy bunch was a visitation during which no one set foot in the coffee lounge. That crowd did what they were supposed to do—sign the register, offer words of sympathy to the family, view the deceased, and leave quietly. But when serving and opening one's facility to the public, those from all walks of life (and upbringings) will show up at your door.

One evening I happened upon a woman rummaging through the lounge cupboard.

"What are you looking for?" I asked from the doorway.

She looked up, startled. "Coffee," she responded. "I thought I'd make some."

I gestured toward the freshly brewed pot sitting, still full, in clear view on the counter. But like most people caught in a lie, she became even more defensive. "Well!" she huffed. "I was only trying to help!"

Yeah, right.

I'm amazed at the petty thefts that occur. Objects disappear constantly, everything from rolls of toilet paper to entire boxes of tissue (including their decorative plastic covers), scented candles from the women's restroom, ink pens from the register book stand (we now attach pens with a chain), and even the silk floral arrangements that adorn our end tables. We now purchase only arrangements that are too large to fit into any woman's purse.

THOSE FLOWERS ARE LOVELY

Flowers, actually, are another matter entirely. When people arrive at a funeral home, they expect to see flowers. The casket spray, for example, is the traditional large piece of flowers or floral arrangements that rests on the deceased's casket. Priced between $175 and $350, depending on sizes and types of flowers used, it's a big-ticket item any florist is delighted to provide, hopefully with several matching companion pieces to further set the mood—and spike up the tab.

Florists and funeral homes generally enjoy an amicable relationship, since funeral orders comprise the bulk of any florist's day-to-day business and provide a consistent month-to-month cash flow. But some florists are more principled than others. Competing florists have tried to woo me by offering roses to my wife, fruit baskets, or a free spray for every large order I provide. The florist's eternal hope is that the family who runs the funeral home will call for flowers for themselves, and perhaps add those on to a casket spray and its companions. In other words, that way the florist doesn't need to worry about sending a bill and then trying in vain for months to collect on it—he or she will get paid on time from the funeral home.

I have attempted to place an order on a family's behalf, only to be turned down when I requested that the florist bill the family directly. Other pain-in-the-neck florists call me for funeral information when they could just as easily open a newspaper. If I were a florist and the majority of my business consisted of providing flowers to funeral homes, then I would certainly subscribe to all the local papers and scan the obituaries daily. Not only could I quickly confirm the visitation and funeral times, but I could also note the correct spelling of the deceased's name. Families who have to find their loved one's name misspelled on a sympathy card have just one more painful thorn in their side.

There are also rude delivery people who enter through the funeral home's front door during services already in progress with a late bouquet, waltz right into the chapel, and loudly announce their presence. There is no excuse for this. Most funeral homes have a backdoor flower drop-off that they check frequently.

Back in the early 1970s, people sent many more flowers to honor the deceased. Whether he or she was twenty-nine or ninety-nine, the fresh, sweet fragrance of flowers always filled the chapel. We used a panel truck back then (now a minivan) to transport cemetery pieces to the grave site before the funeral procession arrived—typically, cut flowers arranged in papier-mâché baskets or plastic buckets, as opposed to the more elaborate (and fragile) live plants, glass vases, and dish gardens—and our vehicle was always stuffed to the gills.

Today, the quantity of bouquets and arrangements sent is significantly reduced. Friends and even relatives seem to be pooling their resources and going in together on a single basket—so instead of one name on the attached card, there are now seven or eight. Also, today people often send donations to charity in lieu of flowers. There are still a few, though, who give to a charity and purchase a basket, perhaps so they can point out to assembled mourners, "Those are the flowers we sent."

I can hardly believe, however, the conflicts that can arise over funeral blooms, and they're usually from shirttail relatives or people not even related to the deceased. On many occasions, I have had to physically restrain individuals from snatching up live plants and rose-filled vases while the casket is still proceeding out of the chapel. My duty is to deliver the cemetery pieces first, then later the keepers—healthy plants, vases, silk arrangements, and the like—to the family residence. The husband, wife, parents, and grown children should rightfully decide what is to be done with them. But when I question a nonrelative attempting to carry away a floral piece, I often receive a puzzling response: "These are the flowers from my work, and I want them."

I have unsuccessfully tried to explain that, yes, your place of employment may have sent those flowers—but not for your enjoyment. Instead, they were sent as an expression of sympathy to the family. I guess I have yet to compose the ideal reprimand, because I'm so often answered with yet another shameless remark.

DID HE REALLY JUST SAY THAT?

People say things inside funeral homes that they would never say anywhere else in polite society. They'll walk up to a casket with the family of the deceased standing nearby and make remarks like, "Gee, Bert sure wasted away to nothing, didn't he?" Or "How did they get Aunt Jean into that casket, with a shoehorn? She sure gained a lot of weight."

That foot-in-mouth syndrome occurs less often when the deceased is elderly. People seem slightly more comfortable in dealing with the death of an aged loved one—someone who clearly lived a long life, accomplished much, and has gone on to his or her just reward. Otherwise, visitors are so unhinged with the notion of death and the circumstances of their visit that odd utterances just seem to pop out. It's a defense mechanism of sorts, and summoning the right words can be difficult. So I try to give people the benefit of the doubt whenever I hear insensitive comments or spot rude actions. Death is a shock—we don't understand it, and we are never sure exactly what to say to a grieving family. The younger the deceased person is, the less comfortable everyone is. People who die younger than the age of fifty often denote tragedy—a spouse and children left behind, along with many unfulfilled dreams and stunned friends.

Common sense, however, should prevail. I have heard visitors ask in loud, booming voices how the person died. At the visitation of an auto accident victim, people will inquire whether the deceased was decapitated. When a family opts for a closed casket, perhaps because of severe trauma or because that may have been the deceased's wish, there are those who have the gall to ask why. Some even leave abruptly, muttering, "If I had known the casket would be closed, I wouldn't have come tonight."

Suicide cases, always jarring, somehow seem to bring out an even darker, crueler mentality. I have overheard utterly classless individuals ask the family how the deceased did "it": "How many pills did she take?" or "Did he really put the shotgun right into his mouth?"

TO THE CEMETERY...

The funeral procession itself can be an emotional land mine. It is usually arranged in the order of immediate survivors: the spouse, the children, the grandchildren, brothers and sisters, and other relatives and friends. Special parking spaces are reserved for the immediate family, and the rest available are on a first-come, first-served basis.

Several times each year, conflicts develop over where certain parties should be placed in the procession. I've heard many great territorial claims, most along the lines of "I need to be up front; I was his favorite cousin," even if it means riding ahead of a son or daughter. I usually compile a passenger car list as part of the funeral arrangement process, with the order approved in advance by the immediate family. Usually telling a disgruntled mourner that this is in fact the way the family wants the cars lined up quells any disturbance.

The actual funeral procession has become quite an adventure over the years, with passing drivers increasingly preoccupied with their radios, cigarettes, and makeup—combined with today's even more dangerous pastimes of talking on cell phones and even watching television behind the wheel.

As the lead car, I have often maneuvered a hearse into an intersection only to be greeted by angry motorists who give me the finger for holding them up. During mild weather months, with windows open, I've had to listen to some pretty colorful and profane diatribes. The average driver often fails to realize that a funeral procession enjoys the legal right of way and takes precedence over any other vehicle except an emergency one with its lights on. Failure to yield to a funeral procession is a costly moving violation.

I attempt to give as much instruction as possible beforehand to those participating in the procession. I recommend that they turn on their headlights and follow the car ahead of them as closely as safety permits. "Think of it as a parade," I say. Alas, most procession drivers are either too upset by the circumstances or choose not to listen. They lag far behind, which makes for a dangerous situation when they approach a cross street.

Since the grave site is usually the last place where all bereaved family members gather, that is also the place where family conflicts come to a head. A few years ago, I arrived at the cemetery for the burial of the father of two sons. The sons could not stand each other. Neither spoke to the other at the visitation or service. The older one, who had arranged for and paid the funeral bill, requested that I give him the guest registration book, but then the younger one approached me at the cemetery and demanded it.

When I informed him that it was usual to present the book to the person who had paid, he produced a handgun, pointed it at me, and asked for the register book again. I immediately complied with his request and handed it over. I then informed the armed man that I would be happy to return to the funeral home and photocopy the pages for him instead. He agreed, apologized, and put away the gun.

It's not just brothers who act up. A deceased woman was the mother of seven daughters and five sons. Family closeness was severely tested when the youngest daughter had divorced her husband and began a new union as a lesbian. The evening of the mother's visitation proved a strain, with all eleven siblings making derogatory remarks to their sister and her new partner.

The tenseness continued the following day during the funeral ceremony. Not only was the daughter not permitted to sit in the front row with her siblings; her oldest sister began making threats to her sister's partner. We arrived at the cemetery, listened to the minister's words, and proceeded to our respective vehicles. That's when the fireworks started. The oldest sister strode up to her sister's partner and attempted to tackle her. But since the partner was bigger and more athletic, she quickly pummeled the sister into submission—to the amazement of the gathered mourners and myself.

One winter day a few years ago, a large crowd gathered at the graveside of a deceased young man who had accidentally overdosed on various painkillers. Before the minister was able to speak, two inebriated females began to argue. One was a former girlfriend, and the other, his current one.

One accused the other of providing the young man with the lethal concoction that ultimately took his life. As blows began, it was obvious to both battling parties that neither was particularly accurate with punches. So they both reached down to the snow-covered grass and began to pack snowballs to hurl at each other.

Unfortunately, their aim was off as well, so more than a few bystanders were struck in the crossfire. The minister was so disgusted that he quietly departed, leaving me to say a few words over the deceased man's grave.

Drug abuse deaths and their commonality have confounded me for years—not the intentional overdoses, but the accidental overdoses of methadone, cocaine, methamphetamines, and OxyContin. A young couple was recently found dead in their home, both victims of a heroin overdose—I had naively assumed that heroin usage was a 1960s relic. The young couple had left behind three school-age children, whom a loving aunt was to care for.

At the cemetery for the double burial, another aunt, who must have thought she should have been the designated caregiver, felt compelled to create a scene. Drunk and disorderly, she told anyone who would listen that the deceased couple "got what they deserved" for their constant illegal drug use. Finally, another family member asked the aunt to leave. Her response was to get into her car and, on her way out, ram as many of her family members' vehicles as she could.

Another case involving a husband and wife who had accidentally overdosed on OxyContin featured an angry confrontation between two feuding relatives who had supplied the couple with their deadly stash. The mental-midget females each accused the other of furnishing the deceased couple with a big bag of pills on the previous night—but before they could agree on the exact time line, they exchanged blows. One of the brawlers then left the building, only to be followed outside by two other women, who proceeded to beat the first one to a pulp. The scrap was over by the time police arrived, and the two attackers returned to the chapel to brag loudly about their fist-fighting prowess.

Birds of a feather flock together, and that cliché is no more apparent than at the funeral services of deceased drug abusers. Their friends are easily recognizable—skinny from poor nourishment, unkempt from no longer caring about how they look in public, or perhaps so stoned that they don't even realize how terrible they appear. Other adult mourners are rarely teary eyed or emotional, perhaps because they understand the inherent risks of such abusive behavior.

They may also realize that they could be next.

CHAPTER NINE

Those we leave behind

No matter how loving, courageous, or strong we are, we all come into contact with death each time we lose a loved one. Nothing can spare us; nothing can prepare us. We have no idea how we'll respond.

The common denominator among living things is that we all die—as does everyone we love. Yet few of us seem emotionally equipped to deal with death when it happens. Grief sideswipes us and knocks us to the ground like some speeding, out-of-control car. No matter how well we accept the many other logical laws of nature, we never manage to see this one coming.

I cried at my mother's death—and then eventually became resigned that her spirit was in a far better place. Since she saw to it that my siblings and I attended Sunday school and church from the age of three until after high school, exposure to those many sermons at Front Street Presbyterian Church cemented my belief that we go to Heaven after death. When my mother passed, therefore, I felt somewhat comforted by recalling those streets of gold, walls of jasper, and gates of pearl. No more suffering, no more pain, no need for doctors, no need for undertakers— my mother had no doubt earned her heavenly reward.

I still feel secure in that belief, even when the pain of separation gnaws. I rarely visit her grave site, because I know that she is not really there—however, when I do go, I feel a lump in my throat, and I smile as I ponder the huge and lasting impact of her life here on the earth.

Some of us are more stoic than others. Some stand straight; others crumple. Some recover in time; others never do. Some skate to the very brink of madness and then miraculously resurrect themselves. Others fall off the edge and don't come back.

I see them all.

THE MANY FACES OF GRIEVING

When I arrive at the cemetery, leading a funeral procession through the entrance, I often observe a kindly looking elderly gentleman seated in a lawn chair facing a black granite headstone. One day, following a short service, I decided to speak to him.

It was, he told me, a monument dedicated to his wife. She had passed away four years earlier, after forty-four years of marriage. He could not forget her, nor did he wish to.

He would never find anyone else to love, and he had no intention of trying. So he visited her every day, weather permitting. Even on some of the coldest winter mornings he would show up, sometimes remaining in the warmth of his car's interior but still very much present.

He explained to me that he greeted her by name on arrival, settled into his chair, told her of his daily activities, and then said a tender good-bye. Joggers and cemetery personnel steered clear, probably thinking him unbalanced. He didn't care.

To this day, I still wave to him whenever I arrive at the cemetery and as I depart. His genuine smile of recognition—and his enduring devotion to his beloved wife—warm my heart. There are other stories that do, too. A thirty-year-old Nascar fan's monument is decorated with Matchbox cars. His widow and his mother visit regularly. They sit together on a Jeff Gordon blanket and stay a long time.

Sometimes there are difficult stories as well. Once, I saw a grieving father plopped on the ground, his back resting against his late daughter's recently erected monument. I had conducted the funeral for his precious twenty-two-year-old just a few months earlier. At the time of her death, he was an inconsolable basket case—sobbing violently and shaking.

After the funeral he thanked me but admitted that he was thinking of ending his own life so that he might join his daughter in heaven. I informed three separate grief-support organizations, and they contacted the gentleman the next day. One woman who specialized in assisting parents who had lost children reported later that the man seemed to be adjusting well and, in her opinion, was starting to heal.

But the father had already chosen the day of his daughter's monument installation to shoot himself. Cemetery workers noticed him seated at her grave, armed with a handgun, so they called police to the scene. After many tense moments of negotiations and pleading, the father shot himself dead and slumped against the base of his daughter's beautiful pink-granite headstone.

Another time, an elderly woman approached me at the conclusion of her husband's funeral and requested that I escort everyone out of the chapel, so that we might be alone. She then asked me to snip a lock of her husband's hair so that she could retain it as a keepsake. I placed it in a plastic bag and handed it to her.

A few weeks later she stopped by to pay off the funeral bill. She reached into her purse and produced a glass baby-food jar that contained another lock of hair, this one from her child, who had died in 1952. The tightly closed metal lid had kept it in pristine condition for more than fifty years. She also showed me a cracked and faded photograph of her child lying in a casket. She'd made it a habit to gaze at the aged photo and the lock of hair every morning as a tribute—and she planned the same daily ritual to honor her husband.

Another time, my son and I arrived at a beautiful two-story home in an upscale subdivision to remove the body of a young woman, a cancer victim. Bicycles, Big Wheels, and assorted balls scattered about the carefully manicured lawn showed that this was a tragic case indeed: three towheaded little boys, ages four, seven, and ten, had lost their mother.

We entered the front door, and were greeted by the bereaved husband, a red-eyed man of forty. He directed us to the first-floor bedroom, and on the way down the hall, we spotted various family portraits of a beautiful blonde woman, her handsome husband, and their three sons, all smiling at different stages of life.

On entering the bedroom, we met a vision of sadness—the deceased young woman, still in her bed, surrounded by her mother and her children, each tenderly caressing her, and the boys stroking their mother's arms and legs. Their father escorted them out of the room so that we could prepare for her removal. Cancer had reduced this once-lovely woman to a shell of herself; she had sunken, dark eyes, her temples were depressed from severe weight loss, and her limbs as thin as sticks.

We carefully carried her into the waiting hearse, and I consulted with the husband regarding burial plans. As we talked, the ten-year-old looked up at me and said, "Mister, I don't want my mom to be dead."

At the visitation two days later, I watched with great sadness as the devastated family arrived. Then the husband and three little boys stood before the young mother's casket, wracked with grief. Usually, children of that age are easily bored and restless. But throughout the evening, the boys stood near their father, accepting hugs from relatives, yet all the while stealing glances toward their casketed mother.

The father wrote me a kind letter a few weeks later that his wife had been amazingly restored to her original beauty and looked healthy again, just like they remembered. He thanked me over and over for making his wife and the boys' mother look so pretty for her visitation and funeral.

Holiday Heartbreak

For some reason, major holidays are hugely represented at cemeteries. Grave sites are often festooned with New Year's noisemakers in January, heart-shaped red balloons in February, green derby hats in March, and Easter-egg trees in April. I have seen witches on broomsticks and pumpkins of all sizes in October, and cornucopia in November. And in December there are countless Christmas trees, some with battery-powered lights; garlands; icicles; and even small, beautifully wrapped presents.

I have often wondered why survivors go to such lengths. Is it because the deceased loved the holidays? Or does the family want to include him or her in their merrymaking? Such displays may look garish to observers, yet they obviously provide some degree of comfort, or people wouldn't do it. Grief is an intensely personal journey. Each of us handles it in our own way. From 1962 until he died in 1999, the baseball great Joe DiMaggio sent fresh bouquets of red roses twice a week to the crypt of his beloved former wife, Marilyn Monroe.

Never have I seen the holidays more prominent than in the case of a minister's seven-year-old daughter. She was afflicted with erythroblastosis and finally succumbed, outliving her doctor's predictions by three years. She died in late November. This charismatic minister and several of his flock waited for me to arrive at the hospital to take his child to the funeral home. I placed her little body in the vehicle, and the entire group returned to their cars to follow me. The pastor-led mourners even accompanied me into the preparation room and assisted me in placing the girl on the table.

My waiting employer and I soon learned that the assembled congregation planned to keep vigil while we embalmed the body. As soon as the doors closed, they began chanting, wailing, and saying desperate heartfelt prayers—and they continued for hours. I wept as I worked, hearing this heartbroken clergy, his wife, and his friends pleading with God to please bring their little girl back to life. Of course, it was not to be, and even I felt a little cheated on their behalf that God did not answer prayers so genuinely offered.

After the embalming was completed, they handed us the child's burial clothing and hastily selected a casket. We put cosmetics on the beautiful little girl, dressed her, and placed her in a pink casket, its fifty-four-inch length a sad reminder that this was not some ninety-year-old great-grandmother who had lived a long, satisfying life but a vivid realization of every parent's worst nightmare. The progression of events had certainly been unusual. Leading an unofficial procession from the hospital to the funeral home had occurred before, though not often. Embalming a body, however, while family members and friends waited just outside the door was a first for me, as was dressing and putting a dead child in the casket with the mourners looking on. Still, where grieving loved ones are concerned, I always hesitate to make judgments. Perhaps this was part of their healing process. But then, after the funeral, the minister asked us to place his daughter's casket in his car. She would lie, he said, near the family fireplace at home, so she could spend Thanksgiving with the rest of the family. And that's exactly what happened. The day after the holiday we were called back to the residence to retrieve the little girl and conduct a proper funeral service.

The Toughest Cases: Children

There is probably no more heartbreaking human tragedy than for a parent to lose a child. I have no idea what that feels like, and I hope and pray that I never do. With more than thirty years in the profession, I still cannot help becoming teary-eyed at the sight of any parent, wild with grief, standing over the casket of a recently deceased child, young or old.

The young couple that walked through the funeral home front door that morning had the familiar look on both of their faces: reddened and tear-stained eyes, eyes that were swollen and puffy from lack of sleep and a lot of intense sobbing. In contrast, I was very excited and full of joy and happiness that day, as my first child was to be born at any time. Baby Anna was holding out on us, a few days past due, so my wife and I were anxious, and I was playing the proud expectant father routine to the hilt—anyone I saw, whether I knew them or not—was going to hear that my baby daughter was about to be born, and it felt good to receive the congratulatory handshakes and pats on the back.

However, the couple I was about to meet with had lived every parent's nightmare. Their nineteen-year-old son had been brutally murdered—a story I had heard about just the evening before on television news. Two hoodlums had forced their son's car off the road, pulled him and his girlfriend out of the car in a remote area, and made them walk to an abandoned farmhouse. The nineteen-year-old was repeatedly stabbed, and his body was stuffed into a dry well. The two hoodlums forced the girlfriend to participate in the stabbing as well, probably to convince her that by going to the police, she would implicate herself. She was threatened with the same fate should she report the incident to authorities, but she did anyway.

The mother and father told me very little about the manner of their son's death—perhaps it was too painful to recount. We made the funeral arrangements, which included an all-night visitation and funeral service the next day at a large Pentecostal church. We were to take the casket to the church at 4 p.m. and it would stay there until the funeral the next morning. After completing the funeral arrangements, I made the trip to the coroner's office to retrieve the body.

The coroner's personnel were amazed at the manner of this young man's death; they gave me all the gory details the moment I arrived. The chalkboard in the autopsy room reported the grisly findings: the number eighty-eight was scrawled next to the words *stab wounds*. Why stab someone eighty-eight times? The coroner called it a frenzy killing: high on alcohol or drugs, the two perpetrators probably wildly stabbed the victim out of extreme anger or in an attempt to silence the screams of their victim. I had dealt with stabbing victims before, but never with such a number of thrusts. The seasoned coroner's office personnel had never experienced such a number of stab wounds either. The majority of the wounds were introduced into the back of the victim, perhaps because he had assumed a fetal position to ward off a frontal assault. The coroner explained that three or four of the wounds could have been the fatal blow, and the rest were likely postmortem (after death) wounds. My thought then was that I hoped the police would apprehend the two suspects right away.

I brought the body back to the funeral home and placed it on the embalming table. A full autopsy had been performed, so the internal organs were in a plastic bag in the victim's thoracic-abdominal cavity. I removed the bag, opened it, and poured two sixteen-ounce bottles of high-index formaldehyde-based chemical onto the organs to preserve them. I retied the bag and began to inspect the empty thoracic-abdominal cavity of the young stabbing victim who lay before me.

Observing the interior of a deceased human being devoid of life-sustaining organs is awe inspiring, as in "Look at what God has devised for us." There are bony ribs to protect our organs from accidental falls and a massive spinal column that assists us in standing upright. In this case, though, further observation revealed the magnitude of multiple stab wounds. One-inch slices, some vertical and some horizontal, peppered the interior of the young man's back. Knife thrusts had chipped many of his ribs.

After arterially embalming the young man, the interior of the body was dried, and I had to do something to address the huge number of stab wounds in the back, which would cause liquids to leak onto his clothing without treatment. Instead of sewing each wound from the outside, I decided to cover the entire interior of the body with a four-inch coating of plaster of Paris. After the plaster dried, I laid a sheet of thick plastic over the plaster, returned the bag of organs back inside the body, and sewed the thoracic-abdominal cavity together. The next day, the young man was dressed and placed into his casket and delivered to the church for the all-night visitation.

On arriving at the church, I was surprised at the number of police officers present. I was informed that the killers were still at large, and that many times a murderer will return to the scene of the crime or even attend the funeral of the victim. As it turned out in this case, the girlfriend of the deceased man had known the two killers and had given the police the necessary information, but the two assailants were hiding. This case turned out to be one of mistaken identity—the victim was not the killers' intended target. Instead, the victim's cousin had reported the two killers to the police for a minor theft, and the killers had vowed revenge on him. However, they took out their revenge on the victim, not his cousin. The two killers, who were brothers, were eventually apprehended and imprisoned. Perhaps poetic justice prevailed for the victim's family—one murderous brother was stabbed to death in prison and the other committed suicide in the same prison.

With all of these terrible things happening, I still had my own reasons to be happy. I left the all-night visitation and went to the hospital to check on the birth of my daughter. We had quite the all-night vigil as well, and Anna was delivered by Caesarian section at dawn. My sister was and is a labor and delivery nurse at the hospital, and she presented my daughter to me covered with muck. I thought there was something wrong, but she just had not been cleaned up yet. After a thorough cleaning, my wife and I marveled at the beautiful, healthy Anna, who had no hair on her head, which turned out to be a trend with all three of our children. I could easily distinguish my babies in the hospital nursery from any others because of the lack of hair on their heads.

I left the hospital, retrieved the hearse, and went to the Pentecostal church to conduct the funeral ceremony for the young murder victim. Such is the life of the funeral director—welcoming a new life and my own child into the world and thirty minutes later depositing the body of someone else's child into a grave.

When my son Michael was six years old, a family a few streets over from us was in the process of moving to another house in town. The father of the household owned several handguns and stored them in his basement in square milk crates. The family had a seven-year-old boy, and he and his nine-year-old cousin were assisting in the move by carrying small items into waiting pickup trucks. The two little guys came across the container of guns, and like most inquisitive little boys, each armed himself for a make-believe shoot-out. The nine-year-old shot his cousin in the forehead, just above the left eye, with a .38 caliber police special that should not have been loaded. The incident caused lifelong resentment among family members, and I'm sure the boy who lived will never forget the accident.

As I prepared the seven-year-old for burial, I saw many things that reminded me of my own son. The dirty fingernails from a hard day of playing in the dirt; scrapes on both knees, perhaps from falling off of a bicycle or scooter; and mussed, sweaty, and unruly blonde hair. I glanced over at the department store bag that contained the boy's burial clothing—new Teenage Mutant Ninja Turtles underwear and the cutest little suit and tie—items that my own son sometimes wore. This silent little fellow lying on the preparation room table required little restoration for his wound. I inserted a ball of mortuary wax about the size of jawbreaker into the almost perfectly round bullet hole, and then smoothed and feathered it into the natural skin of his forehead. The exit wound in the rear of head was more extensive, but I tightly sewed together the ragged skin of the scalp. When I placed the little guy in his casket, I dropped his head deep into the casket pillow to hide the ugly exit wound.

After an experience such as this one, I hid my only handgun in the trunk of my car, under the spare tire. I hid it so well that when I traded in that particular car for a new one a few years later the gun inadvertently went with the car.

I suppose many families are like ours, not realizing the everyday dangers that can lead to death. Once I realized another danger when I met with an extremely distraught husband and father to arrange for the funerals of his wife and four-year-old daughter. The evening before, the gentleman's wife was relaxing in the bathtub and his daughter peeled off her clothes to get in the tub too. In her haste to climb into the tub, the girl snagged a plugged-in blow-dryer with her foot, and the appliance splashed into the water, electrocuting both mother and daughter.

In my house, we always had a plugged-in blow-dryer resting on the countertop in the bathroom. When my own daughter was about the same age, she sometimes took a bath with my wife. After I talked with the grieving father, I immediately told my wife to unplug our blow-dryer and put it in the vanity cabinet.

This particular case was the first time I was asked to place a mother and her child together in the same casket. I happened to think that it was a nice touch, and I was supportive of the husband. The cemetery, however, was not amused. The cemetery superintendent had wanted to sell the husband two graves, not one. After some negotiation, I convinced the cemetery sexton to go along with the husband. It was not a particularly hard sell—the sexton had a daughter about the same age, so he understood. Since this experience, I have placed a child and parent in the same casket several times.

No matter how old the child is, the grieving is painful. A twenty-four-year-old recent college graduate's car slid on a rain-soaked country road and collided with a signpost. Attached to the post was a square piece of yellow steel with the S-curve warning emblazoned on it. The square was just substantial enough to blast through the windshield and cut into the young man's forehead. He died instantly, with tremendous damage to his face. The car then careened into a ravine, violently tossing the defenseless occupant to and fro inside and causing even more damage to his lifeless body. When I first saw him, the decedent was broken and torn from nearly head to toe, which made for a very time-consuming restoration.

Following the embalming, I encased his limbs in

plastic to ensure against leakage, and then I dressed the entire body in a "union suit," a one-piece, form-fitting, thick-ply plastic garment that covers the deceased from neck to toes. After filling in the traumatic facial and scalp defects with wax, I then glued those areas and allowed them to dry. Because there were so many lacerations, this was a three-hour job then followed by cosmetics and insertion of hair from the back of the head into a wax scalp bed.

After dressing the body and placing him in the casket, I called his parents to see whether they wanted a private viewing to approve of my efforts. They approached their dead son's casket on tiptoes, as if careful not to wake him, and wearing that familiar look of devastation that I have witnessed far too many times. As they neared, their output of tears increased—but strangely enough, there was not a howl or a wail or a scream or a sob. The emotional out-bursts I had been expecting did not come. Instead, both stood hand in hand in front of the casket and stroked their son's hair and cheeks.

I cautioned the mother that his cheeks were freshly waxed and had cosmetics on them, but she didn't heed my warning and continued to stroke her son, eventually rubbing off a lot of my handiwork. She then turned to me and declared that she wanted to see his injuries firsthand. She demanded that I remove the cosmetics and the wax so that she could see for herself the trauma that had caused his death.

At first I was rather irate at such a notion. However, that feeling left me when I remembered that this was her child. How can you say no to the mother who carried him in her body, nourished him at her bosom, changed countless dirty diapers, and endured so many sacrifices and setbacks? If she wished to see what had caused his demise, then so be it.

I excused myself from the chapel and gathered up paper towels and a spatula to begin to undo what I had thought was a triumphant restoration. I slowly began to peel off the natural-looking cosmetics and wax, soon revealing a forehead with a wide gash from the right eyebrow upward into the hairline. When I uncovered the right cheek the result of jagged windshield glass against skin became visible.

After a few more moments, lucky for me, the mother asked me to stop. She and her husband had seen enough. Deep down, I was glad that I would be able to salvage some of my previous efforts. But then I was stunned when the mother told me that she was considering leaving her son unrestored for all to see, especially his friends, so that they might witness the damage that can take place as a result of careless, alcohol-impaired driving.

We sometimes assume that a mother's grief at losing a middle-aged child might be a bit less because an adult child has at least experienced some of what life has to offer. Well, not always. I sat down several years ago with a wealthy seventy-five-year-old widow to arrange services for her fifty-six-year-old son, who was an alcoholic. He had been married and divorced three times, had no children, and was the black sheep of his mother's well-to-do and socially prominent family. The woman was in complete denial about her late son's alcoholism and proclaimed that his liver failure was due to other circumstances. After arranging for an evening visitation, a funeral mass the next day, and selecting an expensive solid copper casket, she revealed that I should prepare for a large crowd consisting only of society's upper crust.

She was correct. At the visitation, the parking lot began to swell with many Cadillacs, Mercedes-Benzes, and even a Bentley or two. Society's best had indeed arrived to pay their respects to a deceased man whom everyone had assumed to be a productive manager with his family's very successful insurance business. In reality, according to associates of the deceased, the gentleman had spent his days in bars, drinking with unsavory associates, and his nights in the furnished condo his family provided.

The moment of truth occurred when some of his alcoholic buddies made their way toward the casket, shook hands with the mother, and remarked within earshot of her friends, "Too bad about Jim, but what did you expect? He was a drunk, just like us." The mother attempted to save face: "You must be thinking of someone else." Surely her momentary embarrassment must have been eclipsed only by the shame she endured upon her next visit to the country club.

Perhaps the most enraging and heart-wrenching case was that of a two-year-old child whose parents were estranged. The child had been in the care of his mother and her new boyfriend, who described the toddler's death as an accident. When I called the medical examiner's office to arrange for the release of the body, the morgue secretary told me that the coroner had ordered an autopsy and was investigating the case as a homicide.

As I placed the cute little scamp on the preparation room table, I immediately recognized the same signs of abuse that I have unfortunately observed far too many times—facial bruising; bruises on each arm that matched the shape of adult fingertips; and two telling, perfectly round bruise outlines on the chest—about the size of quarters and matching the buttons you might see on a child's jumper or bib overalls.

I covered the bruises with makeup and placed the child in a thirty-six-inch white fiberglass casket, larger than necessary to accommodate the toys and trinkets I knew his family would place inside with him. I awaited the family's arrival. The father, grandparents, aunts, uncles, and others showed up en masse, and the touching, familiar cries began. The mother soon arrived with her boyfriend, and the crowd in the chapel parted to allow her access to her deceased son. All the while, those in attendance, myself included, studied her to gauge her reaction. She stood over her child and began speaking to him, asking him why he had to die and saying she was so sorry he had to be in this place. Her boyfriend never left her side and followed her around like a lost puppy.

When I was alone with the mother for a few moments, she asked me why there were cosmetics on her son's face. When I explained that I had needed to cover the bruising, she seemed to be astonished. She attempted to explain what had happened: she was supposedly at the store with her mother while her boyfriend was home alone with her child. On her return, she found the ambulance in her driveway and saw her son being rushed outside. He had supposedly fallen over backward from a chair onto a carpeted floor. Then the story changed to a hardwood floor. Then it changed again. She didn't really know what had happened, because she was in the bathroom at the time, not out shopping at all.

I'm no detective, but it quickly became obvious that she was covering up for her boyfriend. I was puzzled as to why the two were even allowed on the street, since any child's home death is always suspected as a possible murder. I had to commend the child's father for his restraint. I was tempted to allow my old-school neighborhood justice to kick in; take the boyfriend out to the garage; beat him senseless with a baseball bat; and explain to the investigating authorities, "He must have fallen down on the garage floor." But the coward was eventually taken into custody, and from what I heard later, he definitely received his fair reward in prison. Inmates have children too, and they usually despise child killers.

A divorced forty-five-year-old woman wailed and sobbed over the death of her twenty-two-year-old daughter, the victim of an auto accident. The girl had been riding with an inebriated male friend who ran the car off the roadway and into a strand of trees. The impact ejected both from the vehicle. The male was thrown clear and landed softly in the confines of a farmer's freshly plowed field. But the girl flipped in midair and was hurled back-first into a century-old tree trunk. The trajectory and speed of impact tore her heart from its moorings and resulted in her death approximately ninety seconds later.

Except for a few minor cuts on her face from the windshield, the twenty-two-year-old was very viewable. After filling the cuts with wax, followed by some Mary Kay cosmetics, she was easily restored to her former appearance. When I escorted her mother into the funeral home chapel, I could feel her knees buckling and her whole body begin to tremble. She asked for a chair so that she might sit in front of her daughter's casket. But after a few moments of silence, she began what sounded like a chant. She recited, "She's gonna get up; she's gonna get up," over and over, sometimes increasing in volume, as if to summon the Lord above to again breathe life into her reposing daughter.

CHAPTER TEN

That's a nice casket you have there

THE NATIONAL FUNERAL DIRECTORS Association estimates the average funeral bill at nearly $8,000, including funeral services; a steel casket; a burial vault; and certain other items, such as cemetery charges, the obituary, and flowers. Obviously, when limited services are performed or when the customer selects direct cremation, the cost is much lower. But it turns out that a funeral bill is the third largest lump-sum expense a consumer faces in life: you buy a house, you buy a car, and you get stuck with a funeral bill.

Most consumers have a pretty good idea of what they should pay for a home, and most of us purchase cars more often than we arrange for a funeral, so we are fairly knowledgeable about new vehicle prices. So why don't consumers know anything at all about funeral prices? Because we do not want to consider the death of our loved ones. We abhor the thought and attempt to block it out of our minds. "We never discussed death in our family" and "We just never talked about such things"—those are refrains I have heard so many times over the years when I sit down with a family to make funeral arrangements. We are afraid of death and deny it in our society.

After I published my first book, I contacted *AARP: The Magazine* to inquire about running an advertisement to sell my book to their members and readers. The advertising manager told me that the magazine published no advertising relating to death in any manner. I said perhaps "he had his head in the sand" by denying the inevitable. He said the magazine desired advertising that was positive for seniors and that promoting a book about death and end-of-life issues would be too much of a downer for senior readers.

Whether or not it's a downer, at some point we all have to come to terms with what we're going to do with our loved ones.

IT'S NOT A COFFIN

Burying a dead human body deep in the ground has always been the best way to rid society of a potentially serious physical and psychological health hazard. Leaving it outdoors to be ravaged by nature's elements seems repulsive and disrespectful to us. The strong stench, the bloating, the rapid liquefaction, the insect and small animal activity, the rampant bacterial growth, and the possibility of disease have all moved us to dispose of our dead as quickly and efficiently as possible. That usually means depositing the body either several feet beneath the earth's surface or in a tightly sealed, above-ground crypt.

The deceased loved one is the focal point of any funeral, yet much attention is given to the stately steel or wooden container where the deceased is reposing. In most cases, the deceased is nattily attired and posed as if sleeping in a bedlike box designed to look attractive and comfortable. That bedlike box is a casket, *not* a coffin.

In the death-care field, we distinguish between the terms *coffin* and *casket*. To us, a coffin is a wooden box that is wide at the shoulders and narrow at the hips, a style last used in the 1930s. Count Dracula slept in a coffin, and cabinetmakers in the Wild West made coffins. To a funeral director, the term *coffin* is as outdated and inappropriate as referring to an automobile as a horseless carriage.

Today's caskets are mostly the same design as in the 1930s, but they are usually constructed of sheet metal and designed to emulate the look of costly, handcrafted hardwood caskets. An abundance of steel forging and automobile manufacturing techniques have made their way into casket making. Current innovations include more ornate interiors, pinstripes, and special corner applications for the exterior, but the rectangular box of steel, copper, bronze, or hardwood we are familiar with today has not changed very drastically over the past seventy years.

The casket, then, can be constructed of the most rustic materials or the most expensive metals—and anything in between. Just like cars, casket offerings start out as basic squares with few frills and can become elaborately crafted units with velvet interiors and leather-wrapped carrying handles.

TYPICAL RETAIL PRICE RANGES OF CASKETS

Cloth-covered wood	$300–$500
20-gauge steel (non-sealer)	$500–$995
18-gauge steel (sealer)	$1,200–$3,800
16-gauge steel (sealer)	$3,900–$6,500
Stainless steel (sealer)	$3,500–$7,000
Solid copper (sealer)	$4,400–$9,500
Solid bronze (sealer)	$4,500–$17,000
Solid bronze with 14-carat gold plating	$29,000–$35,000

TYPICAL RETAIL PRICE RANGES OF WOOD CASKETS

Selected hardwood veneers	$1,600–$3,400
Solid pecan	$3,200–$3,800
Solid maple	$3,200–$5,000
Solid oak	$2,900–$5,000
Solid cherry	$3,500–$7,500
Solid mahogany	$7,500–$9,500

The cheapest caskets are made of thick cardboard or particleboard and covered with doeskin. Their interiors are fitted with low-grade crepe and cotton wadding, with correspondingly inexpensive pillows. Such caskets are used for both in-ground burials and pre-cremation viewings. They are sometimes referred to as paupers' caskets, as some funeral homes also use them for indigent decedents when they expect little or no payment.

Cloth-covered wood is the next step up, with particleboard covered in blue-, gray-, or burgundy-embossed cloth. The interiors of these are also inexpensive, and sometimes they have a filler of wood shavings in lieu of bedding, which is covered by the interior material. Still featured in funeral homes' display rooms, they serve a useful purpose—they are readily burnable when cremation follows a visitation and they look so cheap that families turn away in horror and instantly upgrade to more expensive models.

The next category of caskets is twenty-gauge steel. Gauges range from twenty, the thinnest, to eighteen and sixteen, the thickest and therefore the most expensive. All twenty-gauge caskets are virtually shaped the same but are available in a variety of exterior and interior colors. As prices rise, trim options increase as well—two-tone color schemes, better interior materials, and even swing bar handles on the outside.

The most basic twenty-gauge is a non-sealer, in which the lid has a small metal catch that attaches to a corresponding hole in the front when closed. In contrast, a sealer casket features a seamless rubber gasket attached to the upper portion of the box. When the lid is closed, a crank is inserted into a hole at the right-side foot of the casket and the lid is closed via an internal gear system that forces the lid against the rubber gasket, thus rendering the casket permanently closed. Some twenty-gauge caskets; most all eighteen- and sixteen-gauge steel caskets; and all stainless steel, copper, and bronze caskets are "sealers." Customers choose sealers more often because funeral directors tell them that the casket becomes air- and watertight, thus forestalling the process of decay.

I have often questioned whether this system accomplishes an actual seal—and the Federal Trade Commission has asked itself the same thing. The FTC now instructs funeral directors to inform families that a sealer casket equipped with a rubber gasket is *resistant* to air and water. At far too many mausoleums in mid-July, I've experienced a pungent bouquet emanating from those sealers. What's more, a sealer casket isn't that important, since nearly all cemeteries require that the casket be placed into a burial vault (more on that a bit later).

The next level of casket, and the most popular one, is eighteen-gauge steel. Most casket sales from the 1970s to the present have been eighteen-gauge-steel selections. Most grieving families do not want to appear cheap, and this medium-priced model fits the bill nicely. I have probably heard the following a thousand times: "We don't want the best, but we don't want the cheapest either. Show us something priced in the middle."

Virtually every color (and combination of colors) is available in the eighteen-gauge selection, as well as interior upgrades, such as velvet, tailoring, and head cap panels (the interior lid panel at the head of the casket), custom-designed with any theme imaginable. Funeral homes generally employ a 150 percent markup to arrive at that retail figure—but I've heard tales of some funeral homes charging four or even five times their wholesale price. The majority of funeral homes nationwide offer reasonably priced, affordable eighteen-gauge steel caskets, and such caskets have become the benchmarks of successful sales.

Today's shaky economy has had a tremendous impact on casket sales. In the 1970s and 1980s, employers used to provide company-paid life insurance, which included coverage for funeral expenses. But today most employers have dropped that benefit. The salad days of the funeral business are gone. Before customers didn't have to worry about how much to spend at the funeral home, and I can recall many occasions when folks stopped by to pay the funeral bill riding in their new car, courtesy of life insurance proceeds. Consumers are obviously more cost conscious today, and a growing majority have to pay funeral costs out of their own pockets. This trend has spawned a great push in marketing lower-cost, twenty-gauge-steel caskets, the thinnest gauge available. The major casket manufacturers are introducing a vast array of choices in the inexpensive line to capture sales of any kind. Extravagant and expensive funerals are on the decline even in traditional Bible Belt strongholds, and many more families are considering what would have been unthinkable to them a generation ago: cremation.

The high-end casket market still exists, though, and it includes stainless steel, copper, and bronze. In the 1970s, the major casket manufacturers, Batesville Casket Company and Aurora Casket Company, encouraged funeral directors to aggressively market the high-end units. They devised ingenious marketing tools and materials for funeral home owners, to demonstrate the durability of high-end caskets to customers.

Stainless-steel caskets, the next step upward, indicate quality, and the eye appeal often more than justifies the price increase. Stainless-steel caskets were touted as the obvious choice of material to wise housewives back in the day—they knew that the same stainless steel was used to make long-lasting knives, forks, and spoons in the kitchen at home. A framed advertising featuring a beautiful apron-clad homemaker was placed in stainless-steel caskets to appeal to women venturing into the casket-selection room. The beautiful homemaker was shown holding a wooden, velvet-lined utensil case to demonstrate that stainless steel was the ultimate material for durability.

Copper and bronze caskets, the most expensive and most profitable sales for funeral homes, have received a great deal more marketing attention than stainless-steel ones. Copper and bronze do not rust. Casket companies emphasize that point in their promotional materials in hopes that intelligent and progressive funeral directors will impart such information to families and push on them the belief that the body contained therein would be unaffected. Casket companies used to provide funeral directors with small copper and bronze samples to display inside caskets so that consumers could touch them and imagine how genuinely protected their deceased loved ones would be. The Statue of Liberty, constructed of copper, was a popular lithograph displayed in caskets to tout copper's durability, as were photos of copper gutters on expensive homes.

Casket companies also advise funeral directors to strategically position an expensive unit right inside the selection-room door. Casket makers recommend that the first casket the consumer notice be a copper or bronze model, because 75 percent of the time, men select the first casket they see. It's assumed that men do this because they like to seem decisive and in control. In reality, though, I think that men walk into the selection room and point to the first casket that catches their eye just so they can get out of the room. Women, however, tend to shop for caskets with a greater degree of deliberation: they compare prices, feel the interior material, ask questions, even lay the burial garments of the deceased inside a casket to make sure the color combination is just right. Mom's periwinkle suit must pick up the navy of the casket's interior; Dad's camel sports coat must match the tan pillow. Yet it's still a man's world at the funeral home; the majority of male-headed households leave the casket choice to the man of the house.

A solid copper casket has been the holy grail sale for funeral directors since the 1950s. I recall as a fifteen-year-old hearing tales of that elusive but finally consummated copper sale. The successful funeral director would be beside himself with pride, relating to his wide-eyed peers just how he'd accomplished his feat: "They were looking real hard at the eighteen-gauge bronze tone, but then they turned around and told me they liked the copper, because it would never rust!"

My supervisor many years ago was a classy, white-haired gentleman, a sharp dresser, and a genuinely nice person. He sold more copper caskets in a single year than anyone I have ever known, and when he did, he would announce, "I sold a copper—again." That pause before *again* was probably a motivational tool to encourage us peons to hawk something better than eighteen gauges.

The same supervisor, held in such awesome esteem by his employees, had a habit of making us feel uncomfortable when we did accomplish a respectable copper-or-better sale. He was rightly concerned about where the payment was coming from, particularly with a high-end product. On many occasions, I had to explain in detail exactly who would pay the bill; whether insurance proceeds were involved; and most important, how soon he could expect the payment. It was always satisfying when

I was able to stroll into his office; report the good news of a high-end casket sale; and hand him the signed contract, complete with an envelope full of cash stapled to it—in other words, a paid-in-full account. My coworkers were sometimes envious of my ability to convince families to pay by the day of the service; however, in most cases, I was merely lucky that I had met people wishing to get it all over with.

Caskets made of solid bronze are the costliest and probably the most impressive looking of all. Bronze sales are rare, though, and when they do occur, most funeral directors are beside themselves with glee. Obviously, as the wholesale cost increases, so does the retail markup and profit margin. Entry-level bronze caskets retail for nearly $5,000 for a low-end and up to $9,000 for a high-end. A gold-plated, solid bronze casket that wholesales for $17,000 sells in some markets for $34,000.

Whenever I travel, I make a point to secure a general price list and a casket price list from a funeral home or two. During a recent trip to Los Angeles, I discovered that one home was charging three times wholesale as common practice. I realize the cost of living is higher there than in Ohio, but that markup was ridiculous.

When I first began my career in the funeral business, solid bronzes were referred to as gangster caskets. From reading about the Mafia and seeing the mobster movies of the day, I learned that a great send-off seemed to be part of their public image. One of the first embalming-fluid salesmen I met was based in Chicago. I always looked forward to his calls because of his spellbinding tales regarding his father's funeral home on the South Side of Chicago in the late 1920s and early 1930s. The father had been approached by a ranking mobster and informed that his business had become the local syndicate's funeral home of choice. When he was handed $10,000 in cash to seal the relationship, the gentleman realized the seriousness of the situation and that he had better play ball.

His first job for the Chicago Mob was to place a bullet-riddled body beneath the bed of a casket already occupied by a recently deceased person. The funeral took place with two occupants, one hidden in the same casket. This act was repeated several times over the years, with a few complaints from pallbearers about the heavy weight they were carrying.

When the practice became too risky, the Mafia partners supposedly equipped his establishment with the South Side's first crematorium. To cremate an enemy and obliterate the body, as my acquaintance described, indicated a total lack of respect. Cremating dispatched enemies was so much easier, with far less evidence left behind, so a whole new cottage industry developed. The funeral director was said to still receive his standard fee for services rendered.

I once drove to a funeral home in Kentucky to bring back an accident victim and I received the grand tour of the small town's establishment. The owner proudly showed me several framed awards proclaiming his funeral home as the top seller of copper and bronze caskets for many years in a row. His casket supplier was no doubt equally excited. What I found most intriguing was that every casket in his display room was either solid copper or solid bronze! No wonder he sold so many. I asked him what happened when a family of modest means came to him for service. He responded that everyone in his area knew that when they patronized him, they had better bring along plenty of money.

The average retail bronze casket is priced at $8,500, so it is not a very common purchase. The few times, perhaps twice a year, that I sell a solid bronze, it is almost an unbelievable experience. That is, I am always puzzled when a customer purchases such an expensive casket. I suppose it is my college sociology taking over, but I want to uncover the reasoning behind spending that much money for an item that you will enjoy for basically a few hours. Is it a guilt trip? Is it to impress the expected mourners? Is it assumed that it is the last thing you can buy for the deceased loved one? Is it the theory that since the cost is so high, it must be the best that money can buy? Does it make you a better son if you buy your deceased mother a solid bronze casket? All of that plays in my mind in the case of such a purchase.

In my experience most bronze sales are not to the ultra-rich but to the middle class. The first time I ever sold a solid bronze was to a retired General Motors factory worker who had saved money over the years specifically for his wife's burial. He didn't trust life insurance sales-people and even opted not to accept the insurance GM offered. Still, he told me he wanted the most expensive casket for his spouse, and he didn't care what it cost. Most funeral homes today have a dedicated room on the premises devoted exclusively to the presentation of caskets, burial vault models, and perhaps cremation urns. The showroom or selection room, with an average of fifteen to twenty units, has always been, and hopefully will remain, a place where the thought of profits dance like sugarplums in the funeral director's head.

Many years ago, I met a funeral director who operated his business in my hometown back in the 1940s. As we discussed our common vocation, he offered for my perusal a brochure he handed out to potential customers back in his day. It was the last brochure he had, so I couldn't keep it, but it described his funeral home as equipped with "ice cold conditioned air," "two reposing parlors," and "a goodly supply of the latest metal caskets." I asked the old gentleman what exactly constituted a "goodly supply" and he replied, "Seven."

I attended a family funeral in Tennessee a few years ago, and of course the funeral home owner and I immediately struck up a conversation to talk shop. He gave me the grand tour of his facility, and I was flabbergasted to see that he had fifty-two caskets on display in his showroom. His funeral home was a huge, grand old mansion, and the entire second floor of the building was devoted to casket display. The funeral director informed me that when he brings a bereaved family into his selection room, he makes the effort to pause in front of each casket and explain each and every attribute of the unit before them, from the price, exterior color, material of construction, interior color and fabric, and hardware description. I told him I thought that his funeral arrangement conference must be extremely lengthy, but he informed me that, normally, by the time he and the family had made their way to the seventh or eighth casket, they had made a selection decision.

I am lucky to be in my part of the country, which is close to the major casket manufacturers of eastern Indiana and allows for next-day delivery. Caskets arrive on the manufacturer's delivery trucks, covered by a quilted drape, similar to furniture delivery covers, to defend against dents and dings in transit. Back in the 1960s, I used to enjoy accompanying my older brother to the train station to pick up special-order caskets from the now-defunct National Casket Company, whose home office was in New York. National was known for its many high-end copper and bronze caskets, and when transported by train, the units were encased in wood-slatted crates for protection. The crates were made with top-shelf pine, and each end was branded with the words *National Casket Co.* I discovered that funeral directors were very careful in dismantling the casket crate, not just to avoid damaging the precious cargo but also because they wanted to salvage the high-grade lumber. I have been told that there is many a funeral home that used that crate material as paneling for garages and basements, and even conspicuously displayed the logo.

Batesville and Aurora Casket companies have developed ingenious touch-screen technology for a whole new casket-selection experience. Bereaved family members can custom design their loved one's casket with the mere touch of a finger, selecting the casket shell, color, pinstripes, corner art, and interior fabric and color. The hands-on family participation generates better sales for the funeral home, but families still want to be able to see and touch a real casket before making their final selection.

CASKET ALTERNATIVES

I participated in a point-counterpoint discussion on a PBS television show recently, which pitted me against an advocate of "green" burial. The gentleman promoting green burial immediately railed at me with stabbing criticism of my practice of "planting dead bodies pickled with formaldehyde in a steel box that shall rust and decay, thereby fouling the water table and poisoning our water supply for generations to come." I attempted to defend my profession by assuring him that the casket is inserted into a concrete burial vault in the grave and that most cemeteries do not infringe on the water table. Not to be appeased, the gentleman presented his case with the thought that all cemeteries nationwide should be forced to set aside a certain area of the grounds for those who desire a green burial. Such a burial entails placing the unembalmed body into a large burlap-like sack, and placing the sack into the grave. In theory, the body would decompose naturally and rapidly and pose no environmental threat to society. There is no legal requirement for a body to be embalmed before burial, unless the deceased is to be shipped across state lines or died from a contagious disease. Many funeral homes, however, do require embalming if you are planning a service that includes a viewing or visitation. Many times during the show the gentleman made sure that his toll-free telephone number and website were mentioned to hawk his green burial sacks. I was happy that the discourse between us ended with the gentleman understanding that traditions in different areas of the country dictate funeral customs. The West Coast differs greatly from my area of the country, which happens to prefer burials in the ground. Also, I think my green-burial rival paid attention to me when I explained that a dead human body in only a burlap sack would be fair game for coyotes and other animals. Unless the body was buried very deep, there is no question that animals would be onto the scent of decomposing flesh very soon after interment. This possibility was one of the earliest reasons for a casketed burial.

THE BURIAL VAULT

The casket does not sit in the dirt in the grave, of course. A burial vault is the box-shaped concrete receptacle into which a casket is placed. The burial vault, constructed of concrete and reinforced with steel, resists the entrance of air, water, and any other elements of the grave.

Such grave liners originated many years ago after some unpleasant incidents following the burials of a few wealthy early Americans. Rich people were known to be buried not only in their finest clothing but also with precious jewels. The gravedigger, perhaps a private contractor or even the undertaker himself, would return to the cemetery under the cover of darkness, dig up the fresh grave, open the casket just wide enough to get a hand inside, and then remove the fancy jewelry and sometimes even gold-filled teeth!

When the wealthy Vanderbilt family buried a beloved aunt in the 1890s, fear of grave robbing prompted the family patriarch to have a wrought-iron fence installed into the grave to surround his late aunt's fine casket. Unfortunately, grave robbers were still able to reach through the wrought-iron bars, open the casket, and remove some precious jewelry from the fingers of the deceased. To prevent robbery, the casket needed to be completely encapsulated.

Such atrocities led to the use of rough wood boxes installed into the grave, placement of the casket into the box, and nailing down the lid of the box. Eventually, bedecking deceased loved ones in expensive jewelry went out of style, so crude wooden grave boxes were still considered acceptable liners. But as cemeteries began to fill up with more and more decedents, Mother Nature taught us that wood did not hold up well underground. Changes in weather, insect activity, and moisture caused many a box to decompose, thus causing the grave to partially cave in. Cemetery caretakers and bereaved family members were not happy with such a condition—the caretaker had to keep filling in the area with more and more dirt, even planting English ivy or myrtle on top to help hide disappearing earth.

Steel vaults soon became a trend. A thick seven-gauge plate of steel was placed into the bottom of the grave; after the casket was placed on the base plate of steel, a dome-like lid was lowered into the grave, and the domed top of the vault and the bottom plate snapped together at six connecting points. The air-seal principle then came into effect. Just as when turning a glass upside down in a sink full of water the air pressure keeps the water from entering the glass, in the air-seal burial vault, pressure keeps water from the casket in the grave. Steel burial vaults were rather expensive, so a lot of people scratched their heads to come up with a more economical way to protect a loved one's casket from not only grave robbers but also the ravages of the elements.

The arrival of concrete ushered in the notion of a manufactured burial box, created by pouring the economical material into a mold to form a tub-like structure and then crafting a corresponding lid to construct a concrete box. Concrete is solid enough to prove an ideal barrier against moisture and other elements. Also, the dirt used to fill an adult grave is of tremendous weight, and with vehicles and other cemetery machinery traveling overhead, a stout burial vault not only keeps the grave from collapsing but also protects the casket and its resident.

A concrete burial box is just what it sounds like—a large grave liner with a lid. The lid is placed on top, where it sits flush with the leading edge of the bottom portion. It possesses no sealing properties and is not air- or water-tight. In contrast, a vault is constructed with reinforced steel rods for added strength, much like a sidewalk. It also carries some degree of protection, since it is constructed tongue-in-groove and equipped with a thick, tar-like seal-ant. The bottom of the vault features the molded tongue around the top edge, and the corresponding groove in the lid meets and somewhat improves the protection of the casket. A mastic of tar-like material is introduced into the groove of the vault bottom to successfully seal the vault. Over time, many innovations have been added to burial vaults to increase their strength and durability, such as rein-forcing the concrete with steel rebar and adding stainless steel, copper, and even bronze sheets to line the interior of the vault. Vault manufacturers have resorted to dressing up their products with such costly amenities as copper, bronze, stainless steel, and fiberglass liners, and even lids decorated with religious emblems and pastoral scenes. As with "sealer" caskets, the Federal Trade Commission pro-hibits funeral homes from warranting results—although manufacturers can choose to do so. Also, because of a lack of training or downright deception, some cemeteries still sell unsuspecting consumers inexpensive, non-protective concrete boxes, all the while referring to them as vaults.

A MAUSOLEUM, OR A MESS?

Elaborate mausoleums—once reserved for the very wealthy—are constructed on cemetery grounds and allow for entombment of both husband and wife, or even entire families. Most folks who select mausoleums do not wish to be buried in the ground, and they assume that a crypt results in a much cleaner disposition. But since heat accelerates decomposition, just imagine the speed of decomposition when the recently deceased is placed in a steel casket, and the casket is slid into a crypt up to twenty feet above ground level in midsummer. Even a well-embalmed body oozes fluids over time, although in a steel sealed casket, it shouldn't present any problems in a mausoleum setting.

Under certain conditions, however, such as a poorly embalmed or unembalmed body, the use of a cheap or non-sealing casket such as hardwood, or shortcuts made by the embalmer or mausoleum operator, some horrific and disgusting events can occur. I advocate the use of lime in any casket destined for mausoleum entombment. Pour a three- or four-inch bed across the entire length and width of the casket's bottom, and any fluids will be totally absorbed. Even sealed steel caskets have small pinholes in the corners, and, of course, liquids follow the path of least resistance. Mausoleum operators should therefore not allow a non-sealing casket of any kind, steel or hardwood, to be placed in a crypt. A few mausoleum operators offer for sale a huge, thick plastic bag that surrounds the casket and is zipped up before crypt placement. A good idea, yet some family members either cannot afford such an option or simply choose not to do so.

I have seen evidence, both indoors and outdoors, of bodily fluids that have leaked out of the crypt and down the wall onto the spaces between a mausoleum's granite letters. Accompanying any leakage is the obvious odor. During the summer months, while conducting funeral services in a mausoleum chapel teeming with that stench, it can become nearly unbearable. Mourners walk through the doors and then look at one another in stunned disbelief, asking, "What's that awful smell?"

EXHUMATION/DISINTERMENT

Digging up a casket and vault containing dead human remains and removing said items either to another location in the same cemetery or to a different cemetery is known as exhumation. Exhuming victims for a second autopsy has resolved many mysterious murder cases over the years. I have witnessed several exhumations over the years. The process occurs more frequently than one would imagine.

We funeral directors can observe firsthand whether a burial vault did its job or whether a casket has remained intact or, even upon opening one long buried, whether embalming was adequate. I have seen varying degrees of rusted-out caskets with no burial vault used and pristine-looking caskets that have been inside burial vaults for more than thirty-five years. In many exhumations the casket is opened and most times the sight to behold is extremely unpleasant. What is left of the human form after forty years in the ground is a blackened skeleton. After the flesh deteriorates and drops off, black mold covers everything in sight, including the interior of the casket. I once observed the aforementioned scene with a notable exception—the necktie of the deceased looked brand new! The suit coat, trousers, shirt, socks, and shoes were all but disintegrated, but the polyester necktie remained in place and was still as neatly knotted as it had been forty years earlier.

Cemetery mistakes are the chief cause of disinterments. Perhaps an old caretaker kept all records in his head, not on paper, and would mistakenly bury someone in the wrong grave. Such an error might not be noticed for months—but in many situations, the family immediately recognizes that their loved one is about to be placed in the wrong grave. Such mishaps are just one reason cemeteries require families to sign for burials before the funerals take place—to limit the cemetery's liability. A significant number of site disputes are probably never settled because families who continue to complain are told that, since they were in such a state of grief at the time of signing, they are to blame for their bad memories and inability to make decisions.

CHAPTER ELEVEN

Let's keep dad on the dresser

CREMATION INVOLVES PLACING A dead human body in a casket or other combustible container, such as a cardboard box, and then placing the container in a cremation chamber or retort, where it is subjected to intense heat and flame. With natural gas burners, both the container and its human contents are incinerated, and substances are consumed or driven off—except for bone fragments and metal, such as dental gold and silver, medical devices, and implants. The remaining non-burnable skeletal fragments are then pulverized in a device that looks like a huge Waring blender. The processed cremains, or ashes, are then placed in a temporary plastic container or urn of one's choice for final disposition—burial, scattering, or placement on the family mantel or in a columbarium niche, a structure designated specifically for the deposit of urns containing cremains. A columbarium is a smaller-scale mausoleum.

Rental caskets are often used in cremation cases. A cardboard tray insert, hidden by overlay material, is positioned in the bed area. After the funeral service, the deceased is slid out of the casket at one end through a drop-down door, a lid is secured on the cardboard insert, and the deceased goes to the crematory. A new interior and cardboard insert are then slid back into the casket for the next occupant.

I have encountered several situations in which people abhored the idea of a rental casket. One man wanted a complete funeral followed by cremation for his late wife. He absolutely loathed the idea that she would be cremated in a simple cardboard box. He wanted to purchase a very expensive solid cherry casket, hold the funeral service, and then cremate her in the purchased casket. That's what we did.

Another time a man requested the same thing. He insisted on being with the body of his partner throughout the entire death-care process. When his partner died, he had followed the hearse from the hospital to the funeral home and had waited just outside the preparation room while embalming took place. Afterward, the decedent was placed on a dressing table, attired in a favorite set of silk pajamas and robe, and rolled into the chapel for an initial inspection.

The next day, the man returned, styled his partner's hair, and purchased a stately solid walnut casket. After the service, he followed the hearse to the crematory and even helped roll the casket into the crematory receiving area. The operator, realizing he had a grieving person observing his every move, made an exception to his usual routine. Normally he would remove the casket lids, knock down the sides and ends with a sledgehammer, and pile the casket material in a corner to be burned on another day. Taking the casket apart down to only the bed on which the deceased is lying allows for a faster cremation and less fuel usage. But this time, the entire casket and its deceased cargo were inserted into the retort under the watchful eyes of a grieving friend.

Cremation is a growing trend that is slowly making its way into my part of the country, where mostly people prefer to be buried in the ground. Casket manufacturers are feverishly attempting to assist funeral directors by developing new profit producers associated with cremation products and services. From fancier low-end cremation caskets to more expensive cremation urns, directors in the Midwest are going through a feeling-out period—trying to determine what consumers deem valuable and, more important, what they're willing to pay extra for.

After attending a few casket-company-sponsored seminars to introduce the newest offerings for cremation, I have to admit to being amazed at the possibilities. There are cremation-friendly caskets with themed head panels, just like those offered on expensive steel caskets; myriad urns, from the most basic to the most elaborate; mini-urns that match normal urns, so that children can be presented with a small amount of their grandmother's ashes; stainless-steel bracelets equipped with small openings to deposit a smidgeon of ashes and cover later with a screw-on birth-stone cap; and even necklaces with mini-urns attached to the chain! I have actually sold many of these products, so perhaps the casket manufacturers are on to something. If they offer it, someone will probably buy it.

I once believed that only wealthy and highly educated people desired to be cremated. The funeral home where I worked as a teenager was the firm of choice for the area's upper crust, and I was often puzzled as to why doctors and lawyers were not given full-service funerals with all the trimmings. I was told that their families, for generations, had selected cremation, because it was simpler and less stressful for the survivors. I didn't buy it. I believed that it was really because the people didn't have time for a grieving period and didn't want to spend any unnecessary money. Perhaps the rich and the learned of my area had brought their death-care philosophies with them when they arrived from other countries generations earlier.

The cremation rate nears 60 percent in the big metropolises of the East and West coasts, but it is low indeed in Ohio, Kentucky, Indiana, and their surrounding environs. I have even noticed that if an economically challenged family in the South is offered cremation when funds are lacking, they respond with disdain or even anger. Working-class people used to consider the idea of cremation an affront. Today it's more acceptable, but still not nearly as popular as ground burial. One contributing factor to this might be its growing acceptance by Roman Catholics, who previously deemed cremation as taboo.

Also adding to the increase is the higher cost of funerals and especially cemetery charges. Grave-space prices, charges for opening and closing graves, and burial vault requirements have increased disproportionately compared to other rate-of-inflation spikes. When a single grave space costs a family $1,500, opening and closing it costs $900, and a required vault costs $800, then the family has to come up with $3,200 before even speaking with a funeral director. Opting for cremation eliminates that charge.

CREMATION OPTIONS

There are three categories of cremation-related services. First is immediate cremation or direct cremation—the body is cremated shortly after death, with no accompanying ceremonies or rites. The body is removed; placed in a minimum (cardboard) container; and after an arrangement conference with the decedent's family and acquisition of proper signatures, the decedent is cremated. The ashes are delivered in either a basic plastic temporary container or in an urn of the family's selection. Loved ones then decide on the final disposition of the ashes—burial, scattering, or even retaining them for the next family death or perhaps a dual scattering.

I have scattered ashes on behalf of family members many times, sometimes with unanticipated snafus. An avid fisherman passed away recently, and his children wanted his ashes scattered in the nearby river, where he had spent many a pleasant evening. When I handed over the urn, the family asked if I would be willing to accompany them and actually pour the contents into the water. I agreed. But on the riverbank in December, perhaps I should have held the open container just above the water instead of at waist level. The howling wind blew a large quantity of the ashes right back into our chilled faces.

The deceased man's children received that ominous affront with good-natured laughter. Their dad, they said, would have gotten quite a kick out of the calamity. The incident reminded me of the day that Ted Kennedy and his family attempted to scatter the ashes of John F. Kennedy Jr. and his wife, Carolyn, off the end of a naval vessel in the open sea. With high winds and cameras rolling, it appeared that the ashes blew right back toward the ship.

An active elderly lady of substantial means contracted with me for the direct cremation of her late husband of forty-eight years. The day I presented her with her beloved spouse's ashes, she asked whether I would call the office of their favorite golf course to request a scattering into one of the sand traps. This sweet couple had played there in a mixed golf league every Thursday for several years. She even specified the sand trap on the sixth hole, since her husband had been stuck there on several occasions.

I had heard such a request before and in each case had been denied—so I offered her a sneaky alternative.

Why not go out to the course as usual on Thursday with her husband's ashes quietly stashed in her golf bag? Upon reaching the designated trap, she could open the container, pour the ashes into the sand, and use the provided rake to mix them. She called me on Friday morning to report that the deed was done, even though she felt like a criminal the whole time.

With direct cremation, the customer can save hundreds of dollars merely by price shopping on the phone or in person. In my area, direct cremation charges range from a low (at my own funeral home) of $895, including the crematory fee, to a high of $2,495, not including the crematory fee. Crematory operators charge from $180 to $350 to actually cremate the body, and I include that fee as part of my service charge, although most funeral homes do not. Among other states, Florida and California are popular cremation states and are known for conducting price wars for services. Billboard and telephone book advertisements tout the best prices that funeral homes and even direct-disposal operators offer. It is not uncommon to see a billboard in California offering immediate cremation for $395.

Cremation with a memorial is the second category. This is basically the same service as in direct cremation, but an actual funeral ceremony is conducted without the body present. There are extra charges for use of the funeral home or church chapel, an obituary, a register book, clergy, and perhaps flowers. Funeral directors are much happier when a family decides to have a memorial service as opposed to mere direct cremation, as they can make a little more money and an obituary usually appears in the newspaper, which is great advertising. Charges for cremation with a memorial service, like any funeral home service offerings, vary tremendously, so customers should shop around.

The third category is a complete funeral service followed by cremation, which is a growing phenomenon in the funeral industry. The body is embalmed, dressed, placed in a rental casket (or even a purchased wood casket), and a visitation and funeral service are conducted traditionally—the same scenario that precedes a ground burial. The obvious difference is in the final disposition of the deceased. Instead of loading the casket into a hearse for a procession to the cemetery, the family and friends leave the funeral home and the body is cremated in private. This trend is a result of ever-increasing prices that cemeteries charge for grave spaces and for opening and closing the grave. Families have told me that they are happy to have a complete traditional funeral ceremony, cremate the deceased loved one, and not pay between $2,000 and $3,000 to a cemetery for ground burial.

CEMETERIES

Cemeteries are also feeling the effects of the cremation trend and fewer ground burials. To offset the decrease in cash flow, for years operators have sold burial vaults, monuments and markers, and now even caskets. In the early 1970s, funeral directors and cemetery operators began what is now an ongoing adversarial relationship. Directors took offense at cemetery operators' sales of and profits from items that were once their exclusive domain.

When cemeteries first began to sell burial vaults, funeral homes dismissed it as a passing fad. Soon consumers would realize the error of their ways and stop buying products from vendors who had no business selling them. One early problem with cemetery vault sales was that cemetery personnel did not know the difference between a concrete box and an actual sealing vault. And since consumers had even less knowledge, many times a cheaply made fragile box was placed in a grave with the assumption that it was a sealed vault. Funeral directors banded together to try to stop cemetery operators from selling traditional funeral merchandise without a director's license. That attempt went nowhere, and cemetery operators still actively promote burial vaults.

The fact that the cemetery usually stores the complete burial vault outdoors until needed is a thorn in my side. Concrete burial vaults stored in heat, cold, rain, and snow lose significant strength over time and become very fragile indeed. I have seen several cracked, cemetery-provided burial vaults being installed in graves, even though structural integrity was clearly lacking.

Forest Lawn Memorial Parks, in Los Angeles, probably initiated the idea of combining burial and a funeral home in the same location. Memorial parks are cemeteries with either very few or no upright monuments. Forest Lawn takes pride in the fact that there are no upright monuments to clutter the park-like setting, and the beautiful rolling hills attest to that. Flat bronze, ground-level grave markers are barely visible from a distance. You have to walk right up to a grave site to find out who is buried there. For them, it makes sense to have "everything in one place," to quote a 1940s Forest Lawn newspaper ad. "Everything" means cemetery property, crematory, mortuary, and flowers and grave markers available for purchase.

Forest Lawn's founder met tremendous resistance from area funeral homes when he first introduced the concept. However, Forest Lawn prevailed and is the largest such operation in the United States today, and it's still owned and operated by the same family. The combination idea is another one whose time has not yet arrived in my neck of the woods, where the funeral industry evolves at a snail's pace.

THE WAY IT USED TO BE

Over the years, I've enjoyed reviewing the old funeral records at my former places of employment. Dusty binders from the 1950s and 1960s were a favorite research item for me, especially to review funeral costs back in the day. Besides the obvious itemized entries of the time, such as the funeral home service charge and merchandise charges, I noticed that the preprinted records of the funeral often listed a fee for a door badge and wreath. I asked my elderly employer at that time what those things were. He informed me that, many years ago, following the

Victorian tradition, people would affix an intricate black badge or a black wreath on the front door of a home that had experienced a death in the family. Sometimes they attached black bunting to the outside entranceway of the residence to further inform the community that death had visited the home and that proper respect and sympathy was in order. Even today, we Americans still somewhat cling to the Victorian ritual of wearing black as a symbol of mourning. In England in Queen Victoria's time, a mourning widow was expected to wear black clothing for the entire year following her husband's demise. The mourning period for other members of the family depended on their relationship to the deceased and included wearing a black armband. We follow that tradition to a degree today, as when a police officer or firefighter dies in the line of duty and his or her colleagues wear black armbands or a swatch of black tape over their badges. Also, in the sporting world, mourning is displayed conspicuously on uniforms with the deceased player's uniform number or initials.

Another Victorian practice is still found today. In the 1800s, it was common to keep some of the hair of a deceased person, and the practice expanded into an art form. Jewelers of the day would take woven hair of the deceased and design and produce bracelets, earrings, and even watch chains in which the hair was the focal point of the design. Watch chains made of intricately woven hair survive today. I currently grant two or three requests a year for the hair of a deceased person. Sometimes people ask for just a small wisp, and other times they ask me to clip enough to fill a paper sack.

Wearing jewelry constructed from the hair of the deceased is probably the reason for the recent popularity of cremation jewelry that the major casket manufacturers and others are producing. Cremated remains are now "processed," or ground up, much more finely than in the past, to a consistency of white sand, to accommodate the customer's desire to retain some of their loved one's remains. Gold and silver chains that feature a tiny urn or receptacle for cremated remains are very popular today, as are hollow bracelets that can be unscrewed at the ends for a portion of ashes to be deposited inside.

CHAPTER TWELVE

As soon as we sell dad's house, we'll pay your bill

YOU MIGHT REMEMBER THE General Motors factory worker who had saved money over the years specifically for his wife's burial. He wanted the most expensive casket for his wife, and he didn't care what it cost. As we sat at his kitchen table, I saw that the man had no use for banks. I watched in amazement as he pulled $100 bills, one by one, all rolled tightly, from an entire row of old olive jars. Each time he reached $1,000, he asked me to reroll the bills in the opposite direction so they could be smoothed out to be counted. Our transaction complete, I went straight to the bank to deposit the money, which still reeked of olives, as did my fingers. He apparently never thought to rinse out the jars.

WHEN ONLY THE BEST WILL DO

Several times each year, a family demands the finest casket available—and the reasons run the gamut. Wealthy clients, if they don't opt for cremation, insist on the best because that's what the deceased sought in life. Other well-off families are intent on impressing their well-heeled friends and colleagues. They make such remarks as, "Dad always drove a Mercedes-Benz, so we want the Mercedes-Benz of caskets."

Some families assume that the most expensive casket is invariably the highest quality; therefore, they easily justify the purchase. A few look at every casket on display, and then, not finding one costly enough, ask to see a catalog picturing the most elaborate solid bronze or solid mahogany options (every funeral home has such a book on the premises).

A staunch Republican friend recently prearranged his own service and selected the exact same solid mahogany casket of his hero, Ronald Reagan. Another gentleman had just lost his wife to cancer. Before his wife died she had been impressed by a neighbor's casket. The husband asked me how much it would cost, and then requested one that cost twice as much. His wife, he said, always tried to outdo her neighbor in life, so he was going to make it so in death as well.

Another elderly man recently selected an extremely expensive casket for his late wife, reassuring himself that she would have thought it was the "purtiest" one available.

He also insisted that the entire interior be replaced with a quilt design that his wife had loved, even after I informed him that the switch would cost an additional $500.

More than once a beneficiary has informed me, "I have a $25,000 life insurance policy, and I want to spend it all, so there is no money left over for anyone to argue about." Grieving parents also tend to overspend on deceased children. Entering a funeral home often scratches the open sores of both guilt and regret. Even a prodigal child hoping to settle some past parental tiff will purchase a fancy casket to ease a burdensome mind.

THE HAM-BONE OPTION

But just as some consumers insist that money is no object, many more have no desire or no means to spend a lot of money on funeral merchandise.

I once worked for an employer who simply could not understand why a family opted for limited offerings or purchased inexpensive merchandise. "We can't stay in business if we keep selling those tin cans," he'd remark, referring to our low-end caskets. He became especially irate if a family chose immediate cremation—so much cheaper than ground burial—and would be absolutely incensed on the rare occasion of body donation, since our funeral home was merely required to complete a few forms and transport the deceased to the medical school.

A man in the price-shopping mode called one morning and inquired about the cost of our service for body donation. His mother had died, and she had a prearranged agreement, but the son still needed to go through a funeral home to finalize her plans. When I told him that we charged $350 for body donation, he questioned the validity of our pricing and commented that our service in this case was nothing more than a glorified ambulance run. He then wished to speak to the owner. I handed the phone over to my employer—who immediately hit the speakerphone button and instructed me to listen and learn.

His initial tone was pleasant as he explained to the caller that our price included the cost of having two men remove his mother's body from the hospital, the use of the vehicle for transportation, and the secretarial expense needed to complete the necessary documentation. The caller then went into a bargaining mode and asked if we would perform the job for $200. Now steaming, my employer uttered the phrase that would become legendary among all of us for years to come: "Sir, why don't you just shove a ham bone up your mom's ass and let the dogs drag her away?" I was shocked, to say the least. The caller hung up in a huff, and my employer smiled and declared, "I hate price shoppers." From that day forward, if any family ever mentioned that they were short on funds or were looking for our least expensive services, we would all grin at one another and, privately, say, "I suppose we should offer the ham-bone option."

A few of my colleagues still take it personally when a client purchases an inexpensive casket. They see it as a blow to their professionalism. Some are even ashamed to pull a cheaper model out of the hearse, because cemetery personnel recognize quality, even at a distance. That's one reason so many homes position cheaper caskets away from the display area's entrance—they hope customers won't even notice them.

I can relate to both views, to a point. Families will say, for example, "Dad was a simple man; he told us years ago not to waste good money on a casket," or "Mom would come back and haunt us if we spent a lot of money on her funeral." Those things are legitimate in most cases; however, sometimes siblings later tell me that their parents never said such a thing and that their brother or sister just wanted more of the parent's estate.

I have also been in situations where survivors expressed horror at casket prices, demanded to see the least expensive ones, and then turned around and purchased a pricier one than intended because they liked how it looked. Or they chose an inexpensive option and then called back the next day to choose a costlier option because they feared that other family members might be upset.

Another former employer was arranging the funeral of a prominent physician and became enraged when the late doctor's wife requested the simplest casket in stock. He angrily informed the woman that because such a high-profile funeral would inevitably draw a huge, well-heeled crowd, he could not allow her to embarrass herself by laying the good doctor to rest in a "cheapo." The widow relented and selected a higher-priced model—but she told her children that they should call a different funeral home when her time came.

People who aren't funeral directors should understand that we funeral directors, like all salespeople, feel a sense of pride and accomplishment when we hit a homerun, which for us means selling the most expensive casket on the floor. Just as in a real estate office or automobile show-room, the lucky seller is the envy of his peers.

BUYER BEWARE

A few of my colleagues have resorted to stretching the truth and even being downright misleading to avoid selling a cheap casket, especially for obese decedents, who require an oversize (and more expensive) casket. I have heard stories of families being told that the obese loved one can fit only into a certain (very pricey) oversize casket and that there is no alternative. I have also conducted many funerals for families who have been berated for their frugality by competing funeral homes. They come to me because I don't engage in such astonishing trash talk as "I wouldn't bury a dog in that casket" or "You're not really going to put your mother in that sardine can?"

Several years ago a smarmy coworker prided himself on being a casket salesman extraordinaire. He could sell the most expensive units by using some of the oldest, most despicable tricks in the book. He'd drape his arm around a widow's shoulders; stop in front of the costliest casket; and say, "Wouldn't Ed look nice in this one?" or "You know, this is the last thing you can do for Ed" or, "Think of all the nice things Ed bought for you over the years; it's time you paid him back, wouldn't you agree?" or, "You can't take it with you. Have you ever seen a U-Haul pulled by a hearse?"

I am still amazed that anyone could possibly garner high-dollar sales from such inane spiels, yet somehow for this guy they worked. He had, however, an affection for wine, and once was assigned to collect a large unpaid funeral bill that resulted from his having badgered a client with little ability to pay. After making several phone calls and getting no response, he returned to the funeral home late one evening to try reaching the customer at home. He had already consumed a few martinis, and it showed during his conversation. He informed the customer that if he did not make payment in full by the following day, he would go to the cemetery, dig up the casket and vault, and store them both in the funeral home's garage until the bill was paid. The customer arranged a bank loan the very next morning.

Our supervisor was happy with the results but aghast at the collection method. (Luckily the customer didn't initiate an emotional distress lawsuit.) My coworker based his treatment and level of service to a client family on the amount they spent. If they purchased an expensive casket, he would insist that we be extra nice. For a lesser casket, he would ignore them as much as possible. As I said, he was smarmy. I was definitely learning how not to behave.

COLLECTING

Other funeral directors admit to having been terrible businesspeople over the years because of the trusting nature of their enterprise. When a family comes to us in a time of desperation, many of us find it difficult to bring up finances. I always hope that the family mentions money first. Even after three decades, I still find it uncomfortable to question a grieving family about how they will pay their bill.

Some groundwork can be established during the first phone call. My standard inquiry is normally sufficient to give me a clear picture. I ask whether grave space has been set aside for the deceased. If the answer is yes, that usually means a complete funeral with ground burial rather than cremation. A family already intent on cremation usually tells me so at that point. When we later meet the family at the residence, we ask them to bring the necessary paperwork to the arrangement conference, including life insurance policies. If the family has life insurance, that is normally a good sign.

Many insurance companies accept a funeral-home-provided assignment form, which allows the home to assign the proceeds to pay funeral expenses, assuming that the beneficiary of said policy is amenable to the idea. However, in many instances, I have discovered that policies have lapsed because of nonpayment of premiums or the death benefit has been greatly reduced because of loans taken out against it. Other policies have been in force for only a matter of months, and there is generally a two-year contestability clause, which means that the company won't pay off on a policy less than two years old. I have seen some very sad faces before me when I have had to report that the policy the family was depending on is no good.

One Cincinnati-area funeral home was caught a few years ago accepting the total proceeds of insurance policies, even when that amount was substantially more than the stated funeral expenses. On the form the employees would enter "total proceeds" on the line where they would normally write the amount needed. The beneficiary was likely asked to sign a blank assignment form or simply did not read what he or she was signing.

We no longer assume that people have life insurance. Employers tend to eliminate it from benefit packages when cutbacks occur. Customers without life insurance are then forced to work out some sort of payment plan, which usually turns out to be a bad deal for us. Some families request making monthly payments of $100—which means that they can't pay a $5,000 funeral bill for more than four years!

From experience, I can report that such payments are rarely even carried out to completion. An old funeral director friend of mine once said, "The tears dry up when the bill arrives." That adage holds true today. If directors are not paid within thirty days, we will probably not see our money without a fight. We hear many different things: "We're waiting for our income tax refund," "As soon as we sell Dad's house, we'll pay your funeral bill," "We need to sell Mom's car first," or "My aunt in Indiana is sending the money."

A classic consumer ploy is when a family calls one funeral home to take care of their deceased father, and that bill is never paid. Later the mother dies, and the family calls another funeral home, with no intention of paying that bill either. Then, a few years later, Grandma passes on, and that same family calls upon a third funeral home... and so it goes.

We funeral directors have been forced to rethink our credit policies. In years past, if traditional collection procedures failed, we merely waited until someone else in the family died. Then we would attempt to collect on both funerals—or at least on the first one—or we would hope that any family still owing from a previous funeral would call a different home.

As late as the 1970s, few funeral homes asked bereaved families to sign expense contracts. They rightly assumed that the bill would be paid promptly. If not, there was no recourse except for a collection agency or attaching a lien on the responsible party's residence, since we couldn't exactly repossess the merchandise. That's why without life insurance, funeral homes now ask for payment in full before they render any services.

PUBLIC ASSISTANCE

Today there is little, if any, public assistance from cities or counties to pay for funeral costs. Most have an indigent program designed to provide a decent burial for someone with no immediate family. A grave space, burial vault, the opening and closing of the grave, and a grave marker are provided at no charge, and the cemetery bills the city. Funeral homes are instructed to place the body in a "reasonable" casket and deliver it to the cemetery for a brief graveside service. The city then pays the funeral home $500.

Many low-income families who have been in dire financial straits for years or even generations are quick to inquire about any available government assistance. Other poor families scrape together the money to bury their loved ones, without complaining that the city, county, or state should ease their burden. But there have been many occasions on which families have heard of the indigent program and assume that it is there for anyone who requests it.

I met with a young lady recently who sat down to discuss funeral arrangements for her recently deceased grandfather. As I compiled the necessary information, I discovered that all her grandfather's children were deceased, he had no siblings, and the five surviving grandchildren were all he had left. The granddaughter further informed me that the man had no life insurance and was not a war veteran. She then inquired, "Before we go any further, can you call the city and make sure Grandpa is eligible for a city burial?"

I asked her how she knew about such a thing, since most people other than funeral directors do not even know the proper terminology. She explained that when her mother had died a few years earlier, the family had used the indigent burial program, and they had done so again when her sister died months later.

I called the city, and the man in charge asked me to repeat the family's name, which I did. According to policy, he said, he would need to meet personally with the granddaughter to question her about her financial circumstances. The city was changing its attitude regarding city cases; too many families had been abusing the system. Large numbers of sons and daughters were expecting the city to bury their parents for free.

After her meeting, the granddaughter told me that she was shocked and embarrassed when she was asked how much she paid for rent and her monthly car payment. The city ultimately turned her down because she and her siblings all worked, most of them owned homes, and all of them were successfully meeting their car payments. It probably didn't help her case that her family had taken advantage of the city's generosity on two previous occasions.

Social Security pays a lump-sum death benefit of $255. In years past, anyone who paid into or drew Social Security received that amount. The payment was sent to the surviving spouse—or if there was no spouse, to the funeral home providing services. In 1974, the policy changed and the benefit is payable only if the deceased has a surviving spouse or minor children.

The Veterans Administration used to pay $450 for the

funeral expenses of a deceased veteran who served during wartime. Today, the VA makes that payment only if the deceased was drawing a VA pension, was injured in action, or died in a VA medical facility. Many benefits are still available to veterans—free grave spaces in a national cemetery (many local cemeteries also offer free graves to veterans), government-provided grave markers, and U.S. flags. The VA obviously pays the funeral expenses of those killed in action. There are a surprising number of families who have been misinformed somehow that the VA pays the funeral expenses of any deceased veteran. I suppose that when informed that the VA provides a lump-sum death benefit in some cases, some folks assume that means the entire funeral bill is going to be paid.

The state of Ohio ceased its welfare burial award program several years ago. The state used to pay a funeral home $750 to provide a "decent" burial for those who were Medicaid-eligible or for those drawing Supplemental Security Income. At my former place of employment long ago, we conducted several welfare funerals each year, and we saw certain families a number of times.

I was called to the residence of one of our frequent recipient families to remove the body of their late mother. The house was full of children, grandchildren, and great-grandchildren, along with the family pastor. I was asked to sit down and discuss funeral arrangements. On my way into the dining room, I squeezed past a huge projection-screen television. This was in 1987, when the technology involved a large screen attached to a massive cabinet, housing a twenty-inch inverted television and four colored tubes that projected the image onto the enormous screen!

Something else that never ceases to amaze me are the numerous flower baskets that arrive at welfare-case funerals. One might think that senders realize the family is in dire financial straits and would offer money to defray expenses. But we humans are a strange bunch. We love to see things with our names on them. At all funerals, even when an obituary suggests making contributions to some worthy organization in lieu of flowers, most folks do both to make certain that something at the funeral heralds the sender's identity.

My former place of employment used to handle twenty to twenty-five indigent cases each year, which prompted my boss to begin cutting some corners. He decided to use heavy cardboard caskets, normally used for cremation, which featured decorative swirl designs in gray or blue. Lids were attached by large staples, which also served as crude hinges for opening and closing.

Indigent funerals were almost always conducted at the graveside, and we normally opened the casket at the cemetery for the family to view the deceased before the service began. On two separate occasions, I was about to open one of the indigent "specials," only to have a gust of wind blow the lid right out of my hands. I watched in horror as it bounded across the grass and slammed against the monuments, leaving the gathered mourners speechless.

Cemetery personnel and I quickly chased down the wayward lid. Once it was retrieved, I sheepishly replaced it and hoped it would stay secured.

Three Mexican cousins were killed in an auto accident a few years ago, and the family wanted the teenagers sent back home for burial. All three had worked for a landscaping company and were illegal aliens with no green cards and no Social Security numbers. Ohio death certificates, which had to be translated into Spanish for international shipment of human remains, contained spaces that required those numbers. I am certain that the family member who arranged for the funerals gave me fictitious ones, but I had no proof. A translator helped explain to them the requirements and costs involved in international shipment, including airfare for all three and fees incurred by the receiving Mexican funeral director.

The cost for each teenager was $7,000, for a total of $21,000. Since I was concerned about ever seeing the family again, I insisted on immediate payment before any shipment could be made. The following day, one boy's parents brought in a Converse All-Star sneaker box full of hundreds, fifties, twenties, tens, fives, and even ones to cover the entire cost—the result of multiple contributions.

When families reveal to me that they have no money and no insurance, I don't turn them away. Many funeral homes, however, particularly conglomerates, do just that—they simply send them elsewhere. I happen to believe that some relative or friend will eventually come through with funds. So I cut to the chase and simply ask how much they can pay on the spot and then offer whatever service or merchandise will fill their need. Sometimes we eliminate the evening visitation and have a graveside-only service, or sometimes cremation is the answer. Barter is a final option.

BURY MY WIFE, AND I'LL GIVE YOU MY CADILLAC

Back in the 1970s, my wife worked for a dentist who commonly bartered his services in exchange for the services of other like-thinking businesspeople. She once told me about how the dentist had bartered the restoration of an antique car, and the owner of the restoration shop had been in the dentist's office undergoing some quite extensive dental work. One particular day, the dentist instructed my wife to prepare a cubicle for the application of several dental crowns. The shop owner had just finished applying a very expensive paint job to the dentist's classic car and it was payback time! I had never considered bartering with anyone for funeral goods and services until three brothers came to the funeral home a few years ago to arrange for their mother's funeral. The brothers explained that their mother had no life insurance and that all three siblings were in dire financial straits.

After making all the necessary arrangements and arriving at a discounted price, the three brothers asked to be left alone to discuss their options. When they asked me to come back into the arrangement office, they presented a rather unorthodox proposal—they asked whether I would accept a 1996 Ford F-150 pickup truck and a 1997 Ford conversion van in exchange for the selected funeral goods and services.

Since it was obvious that the three gentlemen could not pay for their mother's funeral expenses, I conditionally agreed, so long as the two vehicles were delivered to me for inspection. Later that day, they pulled both vehicles into my parking lot, and I must say, I was impressed. Both had been cleaned and detailed to the point of being twenty-footers: they were sharp as a tack from twenty feet away. On closer inspection, both sported faded paint and extremely high mileage. My son and I drove them across the street to a Ford dealership and requested an estimate of value for each. The sales manager gave us the estimate, which was lower than I had expected, but I agreed to carry out the transaction with the three brothers. I parked both vehicles in my parking lot, affixed a for-sale sign on each, and hoped for the best. Fortunately, both vehicles sold in less than a week, so everyone was satisfied.

Another time, an elderly lady and I had just completed the funeral arrangements for her late husband. She produced her checkbook and told me she did not have the total amount necessary to pay the funeral bill in full. I offered to show her a less expensive casket and a less costly burial vault to offset the price difference, but she stated that she really wanted the originally selected casket and vault. She invited me to come to her home that evening so she could show me her late husband's pickup truck that she had no desire to drive. She asked me to take the truck for the difference in her balance due. I agreed and a gentleman purchased that truck the night of the elderly man's visitation.

Still another time, a middle-aged man sat down with me to discuss arrangements for his recently deceased roommate. He explained that his roommate had allowed life insurance benefits to lapse and that he himself was in no financial position to be able to pay a funeral bill. He further explained that his roommate had recently purchased and accepted delivery of a power wheelchair. He said that the chair had never been used and was sitting on their living room floor still encased in shrink-wrap. The gentleman asked whether I would be willing to accept the chair as payment for his roommate's funeral expenses. Of course I wanted to inspect the item before closing such a deal, so I arranged for my son to go to the gentleman's home to retrieve the power chair. Lo and behold, this motorized wheelchair was absolutely, stunningly beautiful. It was brand new and the seat reminded me of a supple leather bucket seat in a brand new Cadillac. The bright red fiberglass body was gleaming as we plugged the power cord into the wall outlet to begin charging the battery. This power chair was the same one that was being constantly advertised on television. I printed out the product information from a website and was surprised to learn that the retail price was more than $6,000. I called my customer back and informed him that I would be glad to barter with him. In the meantime, my wife was very skeptical about the transaction, and she was rightly concerned about just who would purchase this item from me. I told her not to worry—I would call my many retirement home contacts and request that they put up an announcement about the chair on the home's bulletin board. But I should have listened to the whole commercial I had heard so many times. Because Medicare often pays for power chairs, why would anyone pay me the retail price? After three or four weeks of observing my son drive the chair down the funeral home halls once a day, I gave it to an elderly man from my church who really needed it.

Another time, after a man's funeral I was escorting the new widow back to her car for her trip home from the cemetery. She sat down in the car and motioned for me to come closer. She whispered in my ear, "Meet me at my house about four o'clock this afternoon so I can pay the funeral bill." I was particularly relieved because she had selected very expensive merchandise for her husband's burial and had simply informed me that she would pay her bill the day of the funeral. I started to get a little nervous when she made no offer to pay that morning. I decided to let it go until we concluded the ceremonial rites at the cemetery—I had planned to bring up the bill before she left the cemetery. Armed with a typewritten statement of funeral goods and services and a receipt book, I made my way to her residence. I sat down with her at her kitchen table, and she opened the conversation: "Just how much do I owe you, Mr. Webster?" When I told her that the amount due was slightly more than $12,000, she wanted to know if I would like to see something in the garage. I agreed, and in the garage, she removed a light green cover from what appeared to be a very large automobile. As she carefully removed the cover a foot or so at a time, a 1992 blue Cadillac Fleetwood Brougham began to reveal itself. I once owned a very similar car, and the condition of the one before me was nearly pristine. The lady said that this was her late husband's car and that it had been in the garage for almost a year. Her husband's illness had prevented him from driving, and the car was too large for her. "I know you like Cadillacs," she began. "How about taking this car instead of me giving you $12,000?" Before answering, I looked the car over, opened the driver's-side door, and peered inside—this was a done deal. My only concern was that the car had been sitting idle for nearly a year and sported four flat tires. I told her that I would have a Cadillac dealer tow the car for a thorough once-over. She agreed, and I hastily called the nearest Cadillac agency and anxiously awaited the towing company's arrival. I followed the truck to the dealership, hoping a mechanic would inspect the car immediately. After an hour or so, the mechanic emerged from the shop area and told me that the tires were filled; the oil was changed; a new battery was installed; and all the hoses, belts, and rubber parts were in fine shape. I asked for an estimate of the car's value—it would retail for about $14,000. The sales manager put that figure in writing, and I made my way back to the recently widowed lady's residence to report my findings. I told her about the estimate and offered to pay her the $2,000 difference, yet she would not accept that. She was glad that someone would get some use out of her late husband's car, and she was happy to know that the car would be in good hands.

CHAPTER THIRTEEN

I just switched the heads, and other sketchy practices

A LITTLE OLD LADY enters chapel A, approaches her late husband's casket, and notices that his suit is brown. She tells the undertaker that she had brought in a blue suit for her husband, not a brown one. The undertaker blushes and tells her, "I'm so sorry, Madam, I must have dressed the late Mr. Smith over in chapel B in your husband's suit. Please allow me a moment to rectify the situation."

Thirty seconds later the undertaker escorts the lady back into chapel A. Impressed, the little old lady asks, "How ever did you swap suits so quickly?"

"I didn't," the undertaker replies. "I just switched the heads."

An unbelievable incident occurred many years ago that reminds me of that joke. The inattention of the employees of a large-volume funeral home in my area led to a hugely embarrassing situation. An elderly gentleman was delivered to a church for a visitation to begin at nine o'clock in the morning, followed by a funeral ceremony at ten. The children of the deceased arrived at the church at 8:30 for some private time, and they immediately discovered that the deceased reposing in the casket was not their father.

The funeral director at the church had no idea what had transpired, so he tried his best to smooth things over by attempting a plausible explanation: "Perhaps you have not seen your father in a while," "You know, you are not used to seeing your father with his mouth closed," and "You were obviously close to your father, and in your tremendous grief, perhaps you are not thinking clearly."

The children patiently listened to the funeral director's attempts at an explanation and answered each politely: "Yes, we have seen our father recently," "Yes, we have seen our father with his mouth closed," and "Yes, we are grieving, but that is not our father." The family also stated that the clothing was not that which they had selected.

The funeral director was still not convinced until he slid back the shirtsleeve of the reposing gentleman and spied the hospital-supplied bracelet that revealed the name, date of birth, and Social Security number of the deceased. I'm sure the funeral director's heart sank when the reality of this nightmare sank in. The wrong body had been brought to the church. He apologized to the assembled family members and immediately called the funeral home to have his employees try to find the correct deceased gentleman.

Sure enough, there was another elderly gentleman lying in casketed repose in one of the funeral home's chapels.

By the time the correct deceased gentleman was delivered to the church for his funeral service it was past ten o'clock. I cannot imagine how much embarrassment that funeral director endured in the eyes of the family involved and the entire church full of congregants. Lesson learned: clearly mark the clothing, the casket, and of course the body of the deceased.

People should know that funeral directors take legitimate complaints very seriously. Immediate damage control is of utmost importance, since a family who feels slighted or mistreated in any way will surely call on a competing funeral home for service in the future.

I'D LIKE TO TALK TO THE BOSS

Most complaints, thank goodness, are minor, usually the result of some miscommunication. Obituaries are the most common snags, as when a family member has gone unmentioned or a name has been incorrectly spelled. Such incidences can be smoothed over quickly with no lasting severe effects.

But it's not always that simple. After I conducted funeral services for a deceased friend, I was delighted when my employer handed me a letter from my friend's spouse. I assumed it would be congratulatory, perhaps lauding me for my fine job of caring for her family's needs. But as I read the letter I slowly became shocked at its contents.

She was terribly upset over "many" incidents taking place at both the funeral home and the cemetery. I pored over her list of infractions and decided to call her to go over each one.

She was angry about late arrivals being allowed to enter the chapel. I explained that letting people in after the funeral had begun was customary. She was angry about the chapel door squeaking every time it was opened. I assured her that I would spray WD-40 on the hinges. She was angry about two babies crying throughout most of the service. I explained that such disturbances were common at both weddings and funerals, and it wasn't my place to order young mothers to leave. Her next problem was with the lounge—she was upset that a place where small children played might be filled with cigarette smoke. She was also appalled that a funeral home would charge fifty cents for a can of soda at her husband's visitation and funeral, thereby profiting further at her expense. I happened to agree about the lounge complaints—since then there's no smoking inside my funeral home and I don't charge for coffee or soft drinks. Her next problem was with the cemetery and that there were not enough chairs graveside; typically, cemeteries set up only a dozen. She also disliked the large pile of dirt next to her husband's grave—it's easier to fill the grave this way after everyone leaves.

After several minutes, I realized that no matter what I said, she was not about to be satisfied. I expressed my regret and hung up with a sinking feeling of failure. However, a few weeks later, another letter arrived. Expecting an additional litany of dissatisfactions, I opened it to find a letter of apology. The woman thanked me for everything I had done and admitted that her previous venting was her way of dispensing her anger over her husband's early death. I had just happened to be the target.

THEIR MISTAKE IS MY BUSINESS

As much as I try to rectify my own mistakes, fixing the mistakes of other funeral home directors has meant boons for my business. I am constantly amazed at the number of occasions on which I am asked to remove a body from a competing funeral home to my own. Once in a great while, it is merely a case of forgetfulness on the part of the bereaved family. In a time of immense grief, family members may request that a hospital or nursing home call a certain funeral home and then remember that they had meant to call someone else. Most times families change funeral homes because of cost. Unsuspecting family members are confronted by a high price at a funeral home and decide to halt the arrangement process and go back home to regroup and reconsider their options. Since I pride myself on offering the best price and value, and I heavily advertise that fact, I receive a huge amount of price shoppers—both before and after a death. But price is not always the motivating factor to change funeral homes.

One day, a large contingent of nearly twenty family members came into my office and asked me to quote for them the cost of the least expensive funeral services and merchandise that I offered. I gave them the price and they happily agreed. The person in charge was the son of the deceased, and he asked me to remove his father's body from a competing funeral home to mine. I asked why, and he explained that the original funeral home director that they had met with scolded them for being cheap and told them the casket they had selected was not suitable even for a dead dog. I provided the family with affordable service and merchandise for their loved one.

In another example, the funeral home telephone rang at three o'clock one recent morning. The caller said that her mother was deceased at her residence and asked how soon we could make the removal. I informed the caller that as soon as one of my sons and I dressed and drove to the funeral home to retrieve the hearse, we would be at the nearby residence within thirty-five minutes. That seemed to please the caller, and she handed the telephone off to a hospice nurse who was at the residence. The nurse gave me certain required information and then lowered her voice to a whisper. She thought that I should know that the deceased had died at eleven-thirty in the evening and the family had originally called a competing funeral home for service. Two hours passed and the original funeral home personnel had still not arrived at the residence. The family called the funeral home again, and the answering service said they were on the way. Another hour passed, and still no funeral home. The hospice nurse knew me and suggested to the family that they might want to call me. The funeral home they first called uses a trade service company that performs body removals for funeral homes in the area. The company must have been very busy that night, so busy that it didn't consider a residence call a top priority. We arrived at the residence, made the removal, and were backing out of the family residence driveway when the company's van was pulling into the same driveway.

I don't use an answering service unless it is absolutely necessary. I have a funeral home telephone installed in my home, and with the popularity of cell phones, any phone call can be forwarded to a cell phone. The funeral home telephone never goes unanswered. If I step outside for any reason, the cordless is in my pocket. If I cut the grass, my wife takes over phone duties. When we go out of town, my sons forward the funeral home calls to their cell phones. Phone duty is an inescapable fact of a 24/7 operation.

Cutting corners in the preparation process can have big repercussions. Two elderly sisters came to my door one afternoon and said they had a strange request. Their brother had passed away two days earlier and had been taken to a funeral home that had served their family in the past, but that funeral home had changed hands recently and was now owned by an out-of-state corporation. The two ladies had gone to the funeral home to make the arrangements and had asked to view their brother's body. The funeral director agreed and explained that their brother had just been embalmed and was not dressed, but he offered to allow the sisters to view him in the preparation room. The sisters agreed, and they asked to see their brother's hands. When the funeral director moved the deceased gentleman's hands from under the sheet, the women pointed out that the man's fingernails were just as filthy as they had been two days earlier. They commented to the funeral director that they had assumed such grooming details would be attended to before the body was dressed and placed into the casket. Incredibly, the funeral director took offense and crassly admonished them for telling him "his business." He said he thought the deceased looked fine and that "nobody looks at fingernails anyway."

The sisters left in a huff and came to my funeral home and requested that I retrieve their brother's body from the other funeral home. When I called the funeral director, he protested and told me not to come until he had a chance to speak with the sisters for an opportunity to smooth things over with them. The sisters told him that he had missed his chance to serve them.

Another time, a distraught young lady who had just seen my television commercial called one afternoon to ask me a strange question. She wanted to know whether it was possible to insert dentures into the mouth of someone who had been embalmed. Although slightly difficult, it is possible. She then asked if I would be willing to retrieve her late father from another funeral home, place his dentures into his mouth, and conduct the funeral services.

She explained that her father had died in a hospital the night before, and she waited in the hospital room for the funeral home personnel to arrive to make the removal. The personnel arrived and she related that they were not very compassionate and pretty much hustled her out of the room without giving her a chance to kiss her father good-bye. The next day she went to the funeral home to make the arrangements and handed the funeral director a plastic bag containing her late father's dentures. She told the funeral director that her father was very adamant about having his dentures in his mouth and she wanted to make sure that it was done. The funeral director scoffed at her request and said it was too late—her father had already been embalmed and the dentures should have been given to the funeral home personnel at the hospital.

The daughter protested that she was not given a chance to hand over the dentures because she was practically pushed out of the hospital room the night before. The funeral director held fast, telling the daughter it was impossible to insert the dentures now, but he would be glad to see that the dentures went with her father by placing them in the foot end of his casket. The dentures are usually positioned into the decedent's mouth soon after the embalming process begins. The embalming process firms the facial features thereby holding the mouth firmly closed. It is a bit of a chore to re-open the mouth after embalming has been completed.

The daughter repeated her important request again.

She told me that the funeral director raised his voice and bellowed that he would not put the dentures in her father's mouth. She went home to collect her thoughts and she saw my commercial when she turned on the television.

I called the funeral home to say that I was on the way to pick up the deceased. The funeral director who had met with the daughter was greatly enraged at the thought of losing her family's business. He told me not to come, that he would call the daughter immediately and place the dentures in her father's mouth.

I agreed to hold off until I heard from the daughter— she called shortly thereafter and informed me that the original funeral director had missed his chance to serve her family's needs. She wanted me to take care of her father's services. I removed her father's body from the original funeral home and complied with the daughter's wishes—I carefully placed her father's dentures into his mouth with no problem at all.

Not treating families with dignity and respect can spell a huge loss of business. One morning, a woman called the funeral home and asked if it was possible for me to go to a competing funeral home and retrieve her mother's body so that I could complete the funeral arrangements. I questioned her about changing funeral homes. She said that her mother had died in bed on the second floor of her residence. The funeral home was called to the scene, and two gentlemen arrived to make the removal. The daughter stated that the house was full of family members, including small children and a few neighbors who had come over to express their sympathy. The daughter asked one of the funeral home's personnel about the cost of a funeral and was told, "If you have to ask the price, then maybe you should just cremate your mother."

That comment obviously did not sit well. The mortuary cot would not fit up the narrow staircase, so the funeral home personnel left the cot at the bottom of the stairs and proceeded to the bedroom with a sheet. Instead of wrapping the nude deceased in the available bedding, they merely placed a sheet on her and began to carry her to the cot.

As they made their way down the stairs, one of them accidentally stepped on the sheet and totally exposed the deceased to all who had assembled in the home, small children and neighbors alike. That was the last straw for the daughter. She ordered the funeral home personnel to immediately cover her deceased mother and take her back upstairs and place her back into her bed. They refused and said that, since they were almost out the door, they would take her to the funeral home and call the family later. One of the neighbors knew me and suggested that the family call me and that I would handle the situation with dignity and respect. I did just that.

Of course, dignity and respect mean nothing if you don't have the right body. A young lady called the funeral home one morning and explained that her twenty-three-year-old sister had tragically died and that the body was located in the county morgue. The young lady further explained that the family was of limited means and requested the best possible price I could offer.

After supplying her many service options, we agreed on a suitable arrangement. I assured the woman that I would ask the county morgue about her late sister's release time and meet with her family within the hour. I called the coroner's office to arrange for the proper time to remove the deceased from the facility and was told that no one by that name was there, that perhaps another funeral home had already made the removal.

I replied that the family of the deceased was in my presence, and that they hadn't called another funeral home. "She must be lost," said the representative, in an attempt at some humor. I was assured that the coroner's office would "keep looking." The family left, not knowing where their deceased sister might be and left me wondering the same.

In the meantime, a woman in her fifties was being disinterred from a cemetery only hours after she had been buried that same day. A man who lived next door to the cemetery, and coincidentally had just attended the woman's burial service, noticed the disinterment process, walked over to the grave site, and questioned the cemetery personnel. The gravedigger informed the neighbor that they had buried the wrong person and were digging that person up so the coroner's office could come to the scene and take the body back to their facility. How such news travels so fast, and how the twenty-three-year-old's family heard about the disinterment, I'll never know.

Yet the young woman's sister called me and began to tell me that she knew it was her sister who had been mistakenly buried. I found her story extremely hard to fathom, so I told her I would look into the situation right away. I called the cemetery and was in fact informed that another funeral home had mistakenly retrieved the body of the twenty-three-year-old from the morgue. The other funeral home had been contacted to provide funeral services for the lady in her fifties, but the morgue personnel had mislabeled the pouch that contained the body. The other funeral home did not unzip that pouch to verify identification. So the deceased twenty-three year-old had in fact been mistakenly buried in the cemetery, disinterred, and returned to the morgue.

One of the ways I guard against mistakes is continuity. The funeral process goes like this: the disposition arrangements for a visitation and funeral service or cremation are made; the service takes place, and we head for the cemetery. Myself or my immediate family arranges all the links in this chain. At some of my previous places of employment, the same person didn't even handle certain key events. One person might make the removal, another might arrange services, another might attend the visitation, and yet another might drive the lead car to the cemetery. When several providers attend to events with no continuity, I'm sure the family feels shortchanged and dehumanized. That is why I see to it that either myself or a family member attends personally to all death-care details with any bereaved family.

WHAT IF YOU'RE HIT BY A BUS ON THE WAY HOME?

The funeral industry, like all enterprises, definitely has its share of bad apples. Terrible scenarios abound—from cremating the wrong body to cremating more than one body at a time or even cremating a human and a pet in the same retort and clear cases of taking financial advantage of vulnerable elderly.

A close competitor was caught off guard by a local television news team working on an undercover story about price gouging. The team had caught dubious acts on tape, an inadvertent demonstration of how the funeral director intentionally steered consumers toward expensive high-end caskets in his display room.

Some operators write down license-plate numbers of cemetery visitors, then call them later to sell grave spaces, burial vaults, caskets, or markers. Another ploy is to insist that the entire family of the deceased come to the cemetery and sign a form to verify the grave, even if it has already been owned for many years. Once the family arrives, they attempt to hawk additional graves, mausoleum crypts, markers, vaults, and caskets. In cases of immediate or direct cremation, families are often told that they must purchase expensive hardwood versions—which is not true. Some operators introduce high-pressure, commissioned salespeople as grief or family-service counselors in an attempt to sanitize their image. In reality, they are more like used-car salesmen, and their pitches border on the unbelievable: "Since we are all going to die, you had better buy from us today," or "What if you get hit by a bus on the way home, and you aren't prepared?" Those present might also be encouraged to purchase their own graves right on the spot, so they can "enjoy eternal rest together as a family." If they meet that suggestion with resistance, the "counselor" then scolds the family and acts surprised that they would want their loved ones "buried next to a bunch of strangers."

A memorial park operation in my area has put on some memorable sales-generating events, offering a free Butterball frozen turkey to anyone who comes by to view the property or restaurant gift cards to those willing to listen to pitches describing the newest sections. (As with any major purchase, do not go to a cemetery sales conference alone.) Since people are always happy to accept freebies, another ploy that has worked well is to offer a free grave for any veteran whose spouse has paid full price. Of course, after fees and taxes, full price for the second grave is the price of two graves anyway. The most targeted group is senior citizens, who already are hit hard by phone solicitations for replacement windows, credit cards, and new mortgages—and now cold-calling cemeteries.

The mean-spirited news media love to rake the funeral industry over the coals, and many national headlines are sordid enough to justify scrutiny. The recent crematory scandal in Georgia is one example. An operator was found to be leaving bodies to rot in sheds instead of cremating them because the cremation chamber was allegedly inoperable. He kept the scam going by presenting people with containers of dirt rather than the cremains of their loved ones.

BODY SNATCHING AND GRAVE ROBBING

Part of the reason reporters relish such scary stories is our industry's checkered past—coupled with the fact that we deal with people at their most helpless. In the classic movie *House of Wax*, the proprietor of a wax museum (Vincent Price) is horribly disfigured in an accident, so his hands are not as capable as they once were. Since he is no longer able to craft his wax figures, he resorts to stealing bodies from cemeteries. But the bodies, he discovers, are more decomposed than he would like, so he turns to murder and later retrieves his victims from the local morgue. The fresh kills are then covered in wax, making for very realistic museum fixtures. Perfect horror fare—to the average person, it's believable.

Body snatching and grave robbing were once the only ways for medical schools to obtain specimens for study and dissection. In Cincinnati in the 1800s, one man was notorious for supplying prolific corpses. He would take out his wagon nearly every night to frequent not only small cemeteries but also Spring Grove, the second largest in the United States at the time and the burial spot of many famous Cincinnatians. At $25 per body, he developed quite a business.

Although the authorities were aware of his actions, they did little to stop him until he removed a seven-year-old child from her grave and her corpse was spotted lying in the grave robber's wagon. This act was hideous enough to prompt the state to enact legislation to allow hospitals to solicit family members' permission to acquire their loved ones' dead bodies.

A California medical school was in the news recently for allegedly conducting a scheme to sell human body parts. They removed hearts, lungs, kidneys, and even eyes from donated bodies and retained them in formalin-filled jars for future study. It was discovered, however, that many parts were being shipped elsewhere, still in their preservative states. Other medical schools and even some peculiar individuals were buying human organs.

Someone close to the case reportedly said that private purchasers were displaying the parts on bookshelves as macabre conversation pieces. Someone from New Jersey even requested a complete pristine human brain. It was to be sealed and shipped in a preservative-filled container. But it was packed improperly, and the odor was detected in the shipping service's warehouse. With the return address marked clearly on the label and a small amount of detective work, the jig was up.

Since vital organs for transplantation must be removed before death and under sterile conditions, the organ snatchers were clearly profiting by operating a human chop shop—sort of like stripping stolen cars and selling off the parts.

Some local coroners' offices have been admonished for removing the corneas of decedents without the relatives' permission. And in Cincinnati, a photographer was charged with abuse when he visited a morgue to shoot pictures of corpses holding such objects as keys and musical sheets and then calling it "art." Family members were repulsed—and very angry.

In the early 1980s, I was a member of a committee that coordinated the disposition of mass casualties after natural and human-error disasters. In the three years I served, no such disaster occurred, so I never used my training. But we were shown videos from two separate airline crashes that shocked me—not because of the utter destruction but because of the actions of the first responders.

Some were firefighters and police officers; others were merely gawkers who happened on the scene and were put to work. They were spotted, plain as day, plucking watches and rings from severed arms and emptying cash from wallets. After they jammed the money into their pockets, they tossed the wallets back on the ground to be discovered later for identification purposes.

A more detailed response is no doubt in force today, as such a disaster would be deemed a crime scene and therefore more vigorously secured. Still, I have witnessed many thefts at accident sites over the years, ranging from a police officer snatching a pack of cigarettes from a victim's shirt pocket to actually removing money. The police pull a wallet from someone's pants pocket to establish identity through a driver's license, so I suppose that makes it incredibly easy to make a "withdrawal." Bereaved families have complained to me that they know money was stolen, but they lack any way to prove it. That's why I always make sure that a minister or family member is in the chapel with me at a funeral's conclusion, so that when the casket is closed, anything that is to stay with the deceased stays there—keepsakes, photographs, or money. If any item is to be handed back to a family member, it is done so immediately and in the presence of a witness.

When making funeral arrangements, the topic of jewelry is always discussed in detail beforehand to ensure that all desires are carried out. When meeting with the elderly, I have noticed that they emphatically insist that all jewelry worn by the deceased be returned. Many of them assume that the funeral director is planning to abscond with any valuables. Such atrocities must have occurred frequently years ago, because that concern seems to be paramount in their minds.

Only a generation ago funeral directors were notorious for stealing. One director friend told me that a coworker back in the 1950s earned a substantial living on the side by removing gold fillings and inlaid crowns (the real McCoy back then, not the plated material used today) from the teeth of decedents awaiting burial. He even claimed that the families gave him permission to do so!

I once delivered a deceased person to a funeral home in northern Ohio, and upon my arrival, the elderly owner offered to give me a tour of his facility. As we casually trod through the grand old mansion, he pointed out the impressive curved staircase, the stained-glass windows, and the thick carpet that had been delivered by a London manufacturer in 1949. The tour's end found us in a dark, dingy basement that housed the preparation room and a cubicle that contained shelf after shelf of unclaimed boxes of cremated remains. On the opposite wall were several plastic bins full of bloody clothing. On each bin was a typewritten sheet giving a full description of the contents and how they came to be soiled. Why someone would keep bins full of biohazardous material on their premises was beyond me, yet this gentleman seemed proud to show off his collection. He then pointed to a large box full of old hearing aids and another full of chrome-plated heart pace-makers. He told me he planned to sell the medical devices back to the manufacturers someday and net a tidy profit. I left shortly thereafter, thinking that the guy definitely needed to seek qualified psychiatric help.

DOING GOOD BY THE DECEASED

I'd like to think that my services are on the other end of the spectrum of those horror stories, and the response from my clients bears this out. An elderly gentleman passed away many years ago, and his son, a busy Disney executive and overseer of Disneyland in Anaheim, called me from Los Angeles to meet in Ohio the next day to arrange the funeral. He openly admitted to a blatant disregard for my entire industry, considering all of us ghouls and low-lifes intent on taking advantage of other people's misery. I attempted to allay his concerns, making it clear that any decisions we made that day were not carved in stone and that he was welcome to go back to his hotel and meet with me after he'd had time to think things over. He did just that, and the next morning we arranged for his father's immediate cremation, with the ashes shipped to California for scattering into the Pacific Ocean near Santa Monica.

When I informed the son that his total charges were less than $1,500, he was flabbergasted. His uncle had recently died, and the same services in California had cost him more than $5,000. I responded that obviously the standard of living was much different out there. The man later sent me a nice thank-you note with an additional check for $1,000 and a permanent gate pass for my entire family to Disneyland.

It is gratifying to receive positive feedback from a client's family during and after the performance or our duties in caring for their deceased loved one. Rarely is there a complaint; most always my family and I are showered with compliments and heartfelt thanks from the families we deal with. However, I am extremely amazed at how often one or more bereaved family members actually take the time to put pen to paper and send a card or long letter of thanks addressed to me or one of my sons. I have framed and displayed more than a hundred such messages in the lobby and lounge of the funeral home for all to see.

Others can observe the confirmation of appreciation of our clientele.

There are many feel-good stories in our industry, both local and national, that do not receive any attention. I once worked for a kindhearted man who desired no publicity. Few were aware that every May he would ask the local high school's dean which students could not afford caps, gowns, or class rings. Many participated in graduation ceremonies without ever knowing who their generous benefactor was.

After a tragic accident left seven children without their mother and father, the same man instructed the children's aunt to take all seven to a store and purchase new outfits to wear to their parents' funerals, with the bill sent to him. Of course there was no charge for either of the two funerals. I learned a lot from my employer. Doing good deeds is now my hallmark. I might not be making as much money as some of my colleagues, but I bet I sleep far better.

In October 2004, I noticed a small newspaper article concerning the death of a recently identified thirty-five-year-old woman. A minister was making a plea for assistance with burial expenses. The woman was a known prostitute, and her death was the result of a brutal beating and rape, and she had been shoved out of a moving car and left on the side of the road with no identification.

On a scrap in her pants pocket was a telephone number. The police dialed it and reached a childhood friend with whom she had once lived as a teenager. It turned out that her childhood friend had long ago lost all contact with her. The minister called several area funeral homes to ask whether anyone could donate a casket or a bouquet of flowers. Amazingly, he received nothing.

I listened to his incredible tale; then my daughter and I removed the young lady's body from the coroner's office, performed the embalming, and set out to see what contributions we could gather. I was finally able to obtain a discounted casket and vault, along with a grave space. Township trustees who operated the cemetery agreed to open and close the grave without charge.

The minister reported the good deeds to local television stations, and I was soon deluged with live interview requests. The news reporters seemed shocked that I would perform such a service at my own expense. I was happy for the free promotion and surprised to think that many other directors had the opportunity to offer assistance but did not.

As I've said, I make it a point never to turn a family away because of a dire financial situation. Prices of certain services can be reduced, and less costly merchandise can be substituted to make the death-care experience affordable. I'm sure there are many other funeral directors out there— I hope so, anyway—who assess no charges for infants and offer free services for police officers, firefighters, and military personnel killed in the line of duty. That's typical of most independent family-owned and operated funeral homes, where the hometown director can become a true friend of all community members. Conglomerates are far less likely to reduce prices and outright donations are rare. They also do not wait for insurance payoffs. The corporate brain trust wants to be paid immediately; they think families should be the ones to keep checking their mailboxes.

One time, a truck driver hauling two huge steel coils pulled off the interstate onto the shoulder, perhaps to stop and adjust his cables. One of the coils rolled off the trailer and crushed him. When I arrived on the scene, a wrecker was in the process of raising the coil, precariously suspended by what I thought to be a very fragile cable. I hurriedly assisted in pulling out the unfortunate driver, wanting to spend as little time in harm's way as possible.

I retrieved my mortuary cot and slid it next to the body, which had been smashed from the steel's weight. The poor man had been struck by the steel from his groin area up to his head. His internal organs had blasted out from a tear in his side and lay all around him. It was a surreal scene indeed. One life-squad attendant stared and pointed: "Look, Bob, there's his heart." It was actually a lung.

I transported the body back to the funeral home. As I walked in the door, the telephone was ringing. The Ohio State Patrol asked me to check the driver's pockets; he'd supposedly been carrying more than $40,000 of the trucking company's money. A patrol officer had searched the truck, found nothing, and was resigned to the fact that the money would probably be discovered someday by some homeless guy searching the nearby field for used pop bottles.

I readied a large plastic garbage bag next to the preparation room table to dispose of what was left of the driver's tattered clothing. After peeling away some of his tissue-covered shirt, I happened upon a large wallet with an attached chain, the kind that motorcycle riders carry. I washed off the blood and gore, dried it, and to my surprise found it stuffed full of crisp $100 bills. Briefly, I thought, "How handy to have an extra $40,000!" But I knew the good Lord would not be pleased, so I called the state patrol to report my find.

Shortly thereafter, the trucking company's owner phoned and said he would be at the funeral home the following morning. Upon his arrival, he thanked me for being so honest and handed me a check for $1,000. My name and picture, labeled "Good Guy of the Month," appeared at many Ohio truck stops for the rest of the year.

Another time I was summoned to a stately old farmhouse to remove a farmer's body, which had been discovered in the concrete workshop behind his home, where he'd apparently collapsed while repairing a vehicle. Two sheriffs' cruisers were in the driveway when I arrived, but no one else was in sight. The coroner had told me that the old gentleman lived alone and had two grown sons who lived out of state.

I poked my head through the workshop's door and spotted two deputies counting out cash. One was alternately placing bills in one stack in front of himself and another in front of his partner. They both looked up, sheepish and red faced. An old safe sat below the workbench, its door wide open and it was crammed full of cash.

One deputy remarked, "Well, I guess now we have to include you in the count."

"No, thanks," I replied, and simply removed the old farmer's body and left.

CHAPTER FOURTEEN

The carpetbagger conglomerate

I REALIZED YEARS AGO that the death-care industry needed to change. But unlike the electronics and automobile industries, where explosive updates tend to take place regularly, the funeral business moves with glacier-like slowness, if at all. Although more funeral homes are now modern one-floor facilities, most are still converted two- or three-story residences where business takes place downstairs and the owner and his family live upstairs. Baby boomers in particular have grown tired of those older homes with too many steps leading to the entrances, threadbare "movie theater" carpeting, tiny chapel areas, minimal parking, and staff not open to anything but solemn and predictable services. I have worked at places with no handicap accessibility and with lots so small that visitors were forced to return later when the crowd had diminished or risk parking in a dark alley. I know these things are important, because I actually receive calls in advance to inquire about such things.

MCFUNERAL HOME

A major change, however, in the death-care industry is the corporate buyout. The funeral industry was ripe for such takeovers. Undertakers once handed their businesses to their sons or daughters or transferred ownership through bank loans to trusted employees. Those days are gone. Owners and their families now realize the cash cows they are sitting on. Even grown children who don't want to follow in their parents' footsteps still want to see them get top dollar. A suitcase full of cash can be a powerful persuader.

In the late 1960s, a Texas funeral home owner decided to buy out his city's other two big-volume homes, become top dog, and stop worrying about competition. The plan in its original form was sound: pool the expensive vehicles, retain current employees for continuity's sake, and keep the original names of the two newly acquired businesses so the public wouldn't see any change. Sudden acquisitions usually work well in large cities, where people feel no loyalty and couldn't care less who the owners are. Small towns and suburbs are different. People are far more concerned about who is caring for their deceased loved ones. They want to deal with someone they know from church or Rotary Club—perhaps even a former classmate. They want to see the funeral directors them-selves, or at least their kids, when making arrangements. They also want the funeral director at the visitation, and they want him or her to drive Grandma to the cemetery.

But this owner was not happy with just three funeral homes. He soon began acquiring the largest ones in several neighboring cities as well, often overpaying owners to entice them to sell. Enter the carpetbagger concept. *Carpetbagger* is the word we funeral directors use to describe oppor-tunists who have infiltrated our territory. It has a his-torical relevance; during post–Civil War Reconstruction, Northerners intent on making personal gain headed South and carried their belongings in carpet-covered satchels.

Have You Been Invaded?

How can you tell when carpetbaggers have invaded your area? First, a marketing staff at the conglomerate's faraway home office bombards the affected community with direct-mail pieces aimed at homeowners in the demographic of age forty-five and up. Letters begin something like this: "We need your help! Please take a few moments of your time to assist us in determining what is important to you, the consumer, by answering the following questions: Do you currently own cemetery property? If so, where? How much do your funerals cost? Do you prefer cremation? Do you currently have life insurance?" At the bottom of the form is a perforated card for the addressee to return post-age free. The direct-mail piece is also emblazoned with the recently purchased funeral home's address so that people assume it comes from a familiar business in town.

Responses are followed by phone calls to set up appointments with the corporate funeral home's eager staff of "grief counselors" to sell prepaid insurance policies. Whether or not people return responses, all targeted consumers receive cold calls from hard-sell telephone solicitors (usually at dinnertime), thus reducing the funeral home's credibility equal to that of telemarketers who hawk replacement windows.

Conglomerates have also trolled for potential customers by calling everyone who attends a visitation and has signed the register book. I met a woman who was responsible for deciphering sloppy handwriting, looking up names in the telephone directory, and then calling them to say, "Since you were just at a visitation at our Big Corporation Funeral Home, I'm sure you enjoyed our facility and would probably like to have your own funeral here someday. Perhaps one of our fine counselors can set an appointment time to come to your home, so you can prepay for your funeral."

When a widow is making arrangements for her recently deceased spouse, the conglomerate "counselor" is also trained to "advise" her: "We will draw up the necessary paperwork to duplicate these services, so you'll have a prepaid funeral plan in place for yourself. That way, when your time comes, no one in your family will need to make any hasty decisions under the duress of grief. Sign right here." Since most folks are in the dark about the funeral industry anyway, this ploy usually works, and the still-sobbing widow probably doesn't even realize what she has agreed to.

After a carpetbagger comes to town, the company usually signs a contract with a major casket supplier, such as Batesville or Aurora, and then happily offers a volume discount. Since carpetbaggers purchase far more caskets than family-owned operations, they rightfully receive the discount. However, they don't pass on the savings to consumers. Even the company that I personally feel is a scourge on society, Wal-Mart, passes on savings through their immense buying power. All corporately owned funeral homes and cemeteries in America should probably be discount houses, since they enjoy a tremendous rebate from the suppliers of their most expensive products—caskets.

OVERPRICING AND UNDERSERVING

As I discussed in chapter 11, with an increase in cremation and a decrease in traditional funerals, major casket companies are losing market share. Batesville Casket Company has always told funeral directors that we are much like car dealerships. Consumers must come to us rather than visit an assembly line, and any authorized dealer will do. So once Batesville ascertains the best distribution and storage plan, you will likely see caskets being marketed and sold through Wal-Mart, Costco, or even a stand-alone specialty store.

Right now, however, consumers are learning the hard way that certain purchases are better made from the local funeral home. Corporate-owned cemeteries have increased the price of grave spaces and opening and closing fees to the point of causing an upward spike in the already-increasing number of cremations. Cemetery operators are cutting their own throats with exorbitant fees, and so decreasing the amount of casketed burials. To make up for the loss of income, conglomerate cemeteries have stepped up their attempts to sell caskets, which for years was considered an untouchable product, the sale of which was exclusively a funeral home lock.

Cemeteries could probably pull this off were it not for the unbelievable, unmitigated greed involved. Cemeteries in my area are charging consumers three, four, and even five times the wholesale cost for an item that traditional funeral homes usually charge at most two times wholesale.

One morning a gentleman called, and his first question to me was, "How much is your cheapest steel casket?" I replied $600, and he asked if he could come in right away and see it. After he viewed the inexpensive box, he informed me that he had just left a corporate-owned cemetery and showed me the paperwork for his purchase of the exact same item for $2,650. The casket in question was the exact same casket I had just showed him, and it was from the same manufacturer, which means the cemetery and I paid the same wholesale price: $316. The gentleman was livid at being blatantly overcharged, so I offered to call the cemetery on his behalf and ask about their pricing structure.

The person I spoke to at the cemetery said he personally did not set prices—that was the responsibility of the out-of-state corporate office. He did say that the gentleman in my office would be refunded if he was unhappy with the price. Yet that is the only case in my experience thus far that concluded well for the consumer.

I dealt with a funeral recently in which the wife of a gentleman who had died on a Friday came to me to make funeral arrangements on Saturday morning. When our conversation came to caskets, she lowered her head and told me that she had probably done a "dumb thing." When I asked what, she explained that she and her late husband had been solicited by phone by a cemetery salesperson a few months ago. The salesperson informed the couple that the call was to verify ownership of their two grave spaces. The couple was told that they needed to come to the cemetery and sign a lot-ownership card to update the cemetery records.

Worrying that something could be amiss with their side-by-side final resting places, the couple dutifully went to the cemetery and not only updated cemetery records but also allowed themselves to be talked into purchasing two overpriced burial vaults, a double bronze grave marker, and two overpriced steel caskets. The cemetery salesperson told the couple that cemetery vaults were much better than any offered by funeral homes, that the bronze marker could be purchased only from the cemetery, and that the caskets were priced lower than funeral homes could offer—all of which is untrue.

I looked over the cemetery sales contract with the bereaved wife and let her know that I could provide her with a much better price on all the items she had purchased. She seemed relieved at the notion and asked me to do just that. I called the cemetery and mentioned that the woman wished to cancel the purchase of the vaults, marker, and caskets. The cemetery salesperson transferred me to the manager and I was informed that there was no way they would refund her money.

I had the conversation on speakerphone, and the bereaved woman asked me to hang up so we could speak privately. She hung her head and told me that she had lost her husband and that she was in no mood to fight with the cemetery at this time and to just move forward with the funeral arrangements and the cemetery purchases. I agreed and realized that this is exactly what the conglomerate cemeteries know—when a death occurs most bereaved folks are in no state of mind to dispute a contract. They just call it a bad idea and a learning experience and move on.

BAIT AND SWITCH

Conglomerates used to be wiser about carrying out a proper takeover. They would pay the former owner a monthly or yearly fee to stay on, work the front door, and otherwise make an appearance when appropriate, so the unsuspecting public would assume that it was business as usual. Perhaps the locals had heard rumblings about the funeral home's having been sold—only to be reassured when they saw the former owner ensconced in the entryway. In impersonal metropolitan areas, such a takeover usually goes unnoticed. The Frank E. Campbell Funeral Home, undertaker to the stars in the Big Apple, is corporately owned and operated, but Mr. Campbell is nowhere to be seen. Joseph Gawler's, the premier funeral home in Washington, D.C., serving presidents and diplomats, is also corporately owned. Mr. Gawler isn't there either.

I have a problem with such name retention. It's misleading. Consolidators try to mask new ownerships so that locals will believe that the same funeral home that buried Grandpa is burying Grandma. In Ohio, a law once required that after twenty-four months, a new owner of a funeral home must incorporate his or her surname at the beginning or end of the firm title. In other words, if Joe Jones purchased the Smith Funeral Home, he had two years to change the name of the business to either Smith and Jones Funeral Home, Jones and Smith Funeral Home, or Jones Funeral Home. The law was designed to keep owners from taking advantage of a well-known person's notoriety. Otherwise you could name your business the Jack Nicklaus Funeral Home. Ohio also didn't allow funeral homes to be titled any other way except by the funeral director or owner's surname—no Chapel of Chimes Funeral Home or House of Compassion Funeral Home. Whether because of a payoff by the conglomerates or not, I do not know, but Ohio no longer requires a name change. The original can stay. The business manager must merely have his or her name on a plaque in a visible location.

Just as in most huge takeovers, the bigger it gets, the worse it becomes. A friend works at a home bought for the second time by a conglomerate. He no longer makes any funeral arrangements himself because of severe criticism from the corporate office. Early on, after having faxed a contract for goods and services for review, he would receive a scathing reprimand. He was told he should have upgraded the client family to a more expensive casket and a costlier vault, and he should have recommended the $300 Thomas Kinkade register-book package.

On-site decisions, my friend tells me, are no longer permitted. Even a leaky toilet requires a work order forwarded to the California office, where a district manager dispatches a maintenance technician to troubleshoot. Three labor estimates are required, with proper authorization for any repairs costing more than $100.

Large conglomerates such as Houston's Service Corporation International, Canada's Alderwoods, and Louisiana's Stewart Enterprises, to name only three, have encountered some difficulties when buying up funeral home properties in smaller markets across the country. When they overpay it means that their customers experience price increases to make up for it. I have gained quite a bit of new business from disgruntled families who used carpetbagger homes for previous deaths, only to be shocked at the staggering price increases they faced when they returned there for another family member. Some Alderwoods-owned funeral homes actually lowered their prices at some locations after several consumer complaints and business slowdowns. Alderwoods used to be known as the Loewen Group and is now supposedly emerging from bankruptcy proceedings. Service Corporation International has also been involved in bad publicity, accused of unlicensed embalming in Texas and of recycling graves (reselling those already occupied) in Florida.

Conglomerates are also known for hiring newly licensed embalmers and funeral directors for the obvious reason of being able to pay them less. The funeral industry, like teaching, police work, and medicine, is a place where there is simply no substitute for experience and knowing the answers to questions before they are asked.

Part of the slowdown in recent high-dollar acquisitions is attributed to the fact that many former funeral home owners are tiring of hearing from past customers about their distaste for the new corporate ownership. Smaller town directors are usually happy when a competitor sells out to a big conglomerate. Since everybody likes to tell a story better than the last person who told it, word travels fast when a home is sold. You can bet that the family personnel will tell anyone who will listen that a carpetbagger is now in operation.

Two decades ago, the Federal Trade Commission began an investigation that eventually led to the 1984 Funeral Rule, which forced funeral homes to disclose their prices and to charge consumers for individual services rather than a blanket service charge. That service charge had included removal of the deceased from the place of death, embalming (if requested), cosmetics and dressing, arranging and coordination of services, use of facilities for visitation and ceremony, use of related equipment, transportation to the cemetery, secretarial work and bookkeeping, insurance overhead, and licensing fees. It was imposed on every client, regardless of need, and presented to each family as a lump sum, ranging (in today's dollars) from $2,800 to $4,500, depending on the region. Funeral homes on the East and West coasts generally charged at the higher end. The FTC now requires that funeral homes explain to families how they arrive at their amounts, complete with detailed invoices.

Several incidents in Florida sparked the FTC's action. Florida's funeral homes perform many cremations and more ship-outs than probably any other state. Since retirees from all over America populate the Sunshine State, upon their demise, great numbers are shipped back to their respective hometowns for burial. Tales of families being taken advantage of ran rampant, with reports of full service charges for inexpensive ship-outs to blatantly lying that a casket must be purchased to send a body back home.

Emma Sparkman, an eighty-nine-year-old World War II defense plant worker—a beloved Rosie the Riveter—accompanied a friend to a funeral home in 1983 to assist in arranging the viewing and ship-out of her friend's recently deceased spouse. The two ladies listened to the funeral director's opening speech and decided to select certain necessary services and a nice solid oak casket. They were not informed that they could simply have had the deceased dressed and placed on a table for a final viewing before the ship-out took place. Instead, they were told that for a viewing of any kind, they needed to purchase a casket.

On the day of the viewing, Mrs. Sparkman noticed that the casket was obviously not the previously selected pricey solid oak but some veneered knockoff. On her friend's behalf, she expressed her suspicions to the funeral director, who merely pooh-poohed her concern, assigning it to both ladies being elderly, in grief, and perhaps experiencing fading eyesight. Mrs. Sparkman did not buy this explanation. However, her friend saw no need to pursue things further, chalking it up to one of life's unpleasant experiences. Three years later, Mrs. Sparkman's beloved husband of more than seventy years passed away. She shied away from the previous funeral home and called another in the same city. Her husband was to be shipped home to Delaware for burial, but a small gathering of her peers nudged her into holding a brief visitation. After selecting an expensive navy-blue, stainless-steel casket, she asked the funeral director to please leave the showroom so that she might be alone for a few moments. She took a lipstick from her purse, knelt down, and wrote her name on the bottom of the casket. At the viewing the next day, although heartbroken and grief stricken, she thoroughly inspected the casket again.

Sure enough, the same bait-and-switch had occurred. The blue model containing her husband Vernon was in no way of the same quality as the one shown to her just the day before. The finish was duller, the handles were different, and the interior was not velvet but a lesser-quality crepe—with no sign of the clandestinely applied lipstick signature underneath. Mrs. Sparkman asked the funeral director to roll the original into the chapel so that the two sat side by side. Even with poor eyesight, all assembled could recognize what had taken place, and Mrs. Sparkman was informed there would be no charge for either the casket or the services.

TO OUR CUSTOMERS

"The goods and services shown in this general price list are those we can provide to our customers. You may choose only the items you desire. However, any funeral arrangements you select include a charge for our basic services and overhead. If legal or other requirements mean that you must purchase an item you did not specifically ask for, we will explain the reason in writing on the statement we provide describing the funeral goods and services you selected." These words (or similar words to that effect) are the approved FTC explanation that must appear on any funeral home's general price list. It also includes what is known as the non-declinable charge, an arbitrary amount that homes generally ratchet up by several hundred dollars more than necessary to cover overhead expenses such as rent, insurance, building maintenance, etc. All others are piecemeal—so much for embalming, so much for a hearse, and so on. The FTC Funeral Rule, designed to shield consumers from being overcharged, did just the opposite; it allowed funeral homes to attach the non-declinable fee to each arrangement.

Since the FTC mandates that all funeral homes must not only disclose prices but also offer a general price list to anyone who asks for it, since 1984 there has been a huge surge in price shopping. That spike has increased dramatically in just the past ten years, as a result of customer dissatisfaction, corporate buyouts, and simply because consumers are smarter but less loyal and merely want to save money.

Former employers of twenty years ago swore that Armageddon had arrived in the guise of the FTC when they realized that price disclosures must be given even over the phone. Some funeral directors assumed that any price shopper was a clandestine "plant" sent by a competitor. One former boss would inform callers that they should come by the funeral home in person so that he could show them the list and explain things more thoroughly. If a potential client did arrive, a tug-of-war of sorts would ensue. My boss would point out certain aspects of the list, all the while keeping his hand on it, hoping the customer would not try to take it with him or her.

If families who have experienced recent deaths would allow trusted friends to shop on their behalf, they would probably realize significant savings. A non-grieving friend is better able to compare apples to apples. A former employer used to instruct us to offer a $500 discount to anyone who called or stopped by carrying a previous offer. "Even if we don't make any money on this deal," he used to say, "that's fine, as long as so-and-so down the street doesn't get it." I have found that price shoppers will become former price shoppers once they feel that they have been treated fairly and have received a great perceived value. A happy customer will nearly always call you back.

I also firmly agree with the philosophy behind price disclosures. Overall, the FTC has helped consumers avoid being gouged. Offenders have been forced to adjust their prices to compete, which makes for a better funeral-shopping experience. If your charges are easily justifiable, then you should be happy to share them. I currently advertise prices so consumers immediately know where I stand. I also happily hand out my price list to all who request it, even my colleagues, and I personally go and collect the same lists from them. But I often have to chuckle at the dirty looks I receive.

WHAT YOU NEED TO KNOW

Arranging for funeral services and merchandise before the need arises is a great concept for all concerned, but I advise a little homework. Inform your immediate family as to your death-care wishes as early as possible, even if they meet your introduction of the topic with disgust. At the very least, decide whether you want ground burial or cremation and communicate that preference clearly. I often meet with bereaved families who have no idea as to the deceased's choice of disposition: "Dad never mentioned it," or "I don't think Mom would want to be cremated, but she never said one way or another."

I encourage everyone to make a decision and then act on it. If ground burial is desired, select cemetery property and purchase it—and be sure to inform your family members. My first experiences with pre-need in the 1970s entailed payable-on-death accounts set up at a local bank. In one case, a retired schoolteacher was widowed and had no children. Upon her death there would be no one to carry out her wishes. So she arranged for her funeral service, selected the appropriate merchandise, and paid for everything in advance. She placed the money in a bank account in both her name and the funeral home's name, not to be touched until appropriate proof of death was provided. Yearly interest more than compensated for inflation.

But in the 1970s, banks were paying up to 9 percent interest, so pre-need accounts only two or three years old accrued far more interest than necessary. That windfall was supposed to be returned to the surviving family or to the deceased's estate, and in most cases, that was done. But one former boss used to instruct me to attempt to "upgrade" whenever a large amount of interest had accumulated in a pre-need account.

The 1970s and 1980s were dark periods for abuse in the burgeoning pre-need arena. Detailed reports of funeral directors pocketing pre-need money filled funeral industry publications. They deposited funds into the funeral home's checking account instead of a separate account and then used them for day-to-day expenses. Upon the purchaser's death, the funeral home would perform the service and provide the merchandise, with no one the wiser.

Problems occurred when a purchaser decided to cancel the prearrangement or wished to transfer the account to another funeral home. The original director struggled to come up with the money, an investigation ensued, and the scam was exposed. Funeral homes received quite a black eye. Insurance-based funding and removal of the funeral director from the mix eventually repaired a lot of the damage. Nowadays, if a consumer has a savings account of $10,000 or a like-value life insurance policy, funding a pre-need through a funeral home is totally unnecessary. Going to a home and prearranging wishes and merchandise and then putting such wishes in writing is an excellent idea to save surviving family members from answering tough questions at a time of grief and stress.

Yet many prearrangement clients prefer to pay up front just so they know that their wishes will be met in the future, and also so that the surviving children cannot deviate from the parent's wishes.

My parting thought on the subject of prearrangements is simple. If you pay in advance, make sure the funds are deposited into an insurance product. Don't let a funeral director or pre-need salesperson talk you into placing funds in the funeral home's savings account. With the onslaught of corporate buyouts, many homes will no longer be privately owned in years to come. Funeral home consolidators are buying out one another's assets constantly—and that includes all current pre-need accounts.

CHAPTER FIFTEEN

Six Feet Under—How real is it?

CLAIRE'S MODE OF TRANSPORTATION was only one aspect of HBO's award-winning series that everyone grilled me about. Would I let my daughter drive a lime-green hearse? Would I let my daughter drive a hearse to school? Probably not—but it certainly made a terrific visual. And as a funeral director, I must congratulate the writers and the technical adviser for having presented a largely accurate picture of a family-owned funeral operation, complete with dizzying dynamics and relationship subplots never before explored on television—along with a small but realistic peek inside a mysterious and fascinating vocation.

As I watched many episodes in the company of fellow funeral directors, we often exchanged knowing glances. Whether a scene concerned feuding families, people on modest budgets insisting on the most expensive caskets, or heartfelt sympathy expressed to the bereaved by Nate and David Fisher, we all agreed: "Been there, done that."

Some of the grittiest details were things that only we would notice. One episode from the fifth season, for example, featured an irate Vanessa storming into the prep room to confront Federico. He was in the process of raising a decedent's leg high in the air with his left hand and holding in his right a set of forceps grasping a white plastic AV plug. Its purpose? To be twisted into the anus and/or vagina of the deceased to seal the orifice, thus avoiding any embarrassing leaks or discharges while reposing. Too graphic, you say, even for HBO? Not at all. First, most viewers had no idea what was going on. Second, for those of us in the trade, it provided a riveting touch of authenticity.

Before *Six Feet Under*, most movies and television episodes depicting funeral services seemed eager to portray their directors as pale, somber, black-garbed super-salesmen far more intent on separating consumers from their wallets than on consoling them. Perhaps that's one reason our image still suffers at times; why people are shocked to learn that we actually have a sense of humor; and why we still deal constantly with absurd questions about whether dead bodies truly sit up, make noises, or continue to grow hair and fingernails. *Six Feet Under* made tremendous strides in not only humanizing us but also conveying to the public our proper place in society as providing a much-needed service.

Nate's poignant conversation with the elderly gentleman who did not want to leave the funeral home after his wife's visitation had concluded was very typical, and a classic scene from the show. Older couples may have lived together for decades. When one of them is gone, the other faces a dreadful emptiness. Nate showed compassion toward someone unwilling to return to a silent house; he simply sat down next to the grieving man and let him talk. Any funeral director worth his salt is, above all, a good listener.

There are comical aspects to our business as well that the show has shown. In one episode, a stripper who was electrocuted when her cat pushed electric rollers into her bathtub tested Federico's breast-positioning skills. Her friends were duly impressed with the lifelike uplift of her assets as she lay in the casket. When questioned, Federico admitted he'd placed a cat food can under each breast. While the idea was intriguing, I'll probably stick to my own tried-and-true method, filling brassieres with cotton. On occasion I've overdone it, but each time, the surviving husband has expressed approval with a hearty thumbs-up or even a wink through tear-soaked eyes.

The series included only a couple of misleading embellishments. First, the Fisher and Sons Funeral Home, like many older establishments, was situated in what was once a grand old residence, complete with its outdated basement prep room where embalming and dressing took place. But the home always seemed to acquire its bodies with amazing speed. In reality, the Los Angeles County coroner performs such a staggering number of autopsies and examinations that releasing even a single body could take several days to a week. Nate, David, or Federico would not likely drop by on the very day of someone's death and return home that evening with the decedent already in tow.

Also, David's fear that Mitzi, representing the scary, deep-pocketed corporation, might buy out the competitor down the street and eventually put the Fishers out of business was probably regional. Perhaps in Southern California there is less personalization and therefore less loyalty. In the East and Midwest, however, funeral directors are often trusted friends who secure much of their continued business through word of mouth. If a family-owned home sells to a faceless, out-of-state consolidator, then area consumers hear about it and become understandably skittish about handing over their beloved family members to total strangers.

I would have enjoyed seeing at least one episode that dealt with the inevitable hustle and bustle of a funeral home's busy streak. Several days filled with nonstop and breakneck arrangements, embalming, dressing bodies and placing them in caskets, and then hoping everything had been attended to properly and would run smoothly. Oddly, no one ever seemed to be fully present at what eventually became the Fisher and Diaz Home. I can't help wondering who answered the telephone, who greeted walk-ins, and who sat down with those wishing to learn more about pre-need contracts.

Years ago, some of my friends expressed horror at the prospect of a television series dealing with the death-care industry. Four seasons later, those same people couldn't get enough of it. Creatively, you could hardly do better than to begin each episode with a death—followed by a conference with the decedent's family and some sort of off-the-wall request or unique confrontation. Thanks to *Six Feet Under*, no individual's preference will ever again seem too bizarre. No flare-up among relatives will ever take anyone by surprise. And best of all, every viewing room will forever be known as Casketeria.

The final episode was surprisingly disturbing to some of my friends and family members, but I found the scenes depicting how each main character died both touching and reassuring. After all, we can't deny the fact that each of us will someday expire, and we can't possibly know when. Most reassuring of all was that several earlier episodes made clear the possibility that the main characters might not survive Nate's death. For weeks it seemed apparent that Ruth, David, Claire, George, and Brenda were all losing their grips on reality.

But just as in the many thousands of cases that I have observed, they peered over that cliff into an emotional abyss and decided not to jump. Instead, they backed away and reclaimed their inherent strength, along with their own lives. Finally, they united to toast Nate rather than continue to mourn him.

Life went on. Just as it does, however miraculously, for most of us grieving for those we love and have lost.

⁘ AFTERWORD ⁘

You sound just like him
by Michael Webster

ONE DAY WHEN I was about twelve, my dad came home boasting of a pocketful of change he had won at poker. Apparently, when there was nothing to do at the funeral home where he was employed, he and his coworkers would while away the afternoon playing cards. As he described the various hands that had made him that day's "big wiener," as he put it, I couldn't help thinking that anyone who played games while on the clock must have one terrific deal. "That," I told myself, "is the job for me."

More seeds were planted each time Dad brought home yet another gruesome tale of unidentifiable remains and proceeded to tell it at our dinner table. Although he had my rapt attention, my mom wasn't exactly thrilled. As I grew older, Dad began taking me outside on the porch whenever he felt the urge to describe one more eyebrow-raising story about his day.

Around the time I decided to attend college to major in mortuary science, my dad was experiencing the itch to stop working for the man and become the man himself. In 2001, he opened his own funeral home and was finally able to run things as he saw fit. By then, I was completely aware that history would repeat itself. I would, like him, set myself up for years, perhaps decades, of working for somebody else—but at least it would be my own father. How hard could it be?

What I didn't yet realize, of course, was that Dad would hold me to far higher standards than he would any other employee. Even today, regardless of whether we're embalming, dressing, or just cleaning up, if things do not take place in the manner or sequence that my father expects, then everything I have done is for naught. I've wasted my time—and far more important, I've wasted his. His voice rises to an outside level, even though its only destination is my ears, a mere two feet away.

I have to admit that, on a few occasions, the yelling was justified. My thought process, which darts from one end of the spectrum to the other in the wink of an eye, might sometimes be described as scattered.

A woman phoned our funeral home one day to inquire as to where she might send flowers for an upcoming service. I told her she could just send them to the church of her choice, not realizing that the deceased's family wasn't holding a church service, only brief remarks following a visitation. Of course Dad used his outside voice to proclaim that it was always my responsibility to find out what was going on without assuming anything.

Another time a young woman had passed from cancer, and her cemetery procession of devoted friends and loved ones was extremely long, about seventy-five cars. The first half of the line pulled out of the church's parking lot successfully. But then one car made the mistake of stopping, and oncoming traffic began whizzing by—a serious breach of funeral etiquette, but that's a whole other story. By the time the latter half of the line attempted to get moving, each vehicle had to wait for a traffic lull.

I sprinted down to the highway's nearby intersection and stopped the oncoming cars to keep the rest of the procession together. But I again had made the mistake of assuming wrong. I thought Dad had made a right turn out of the lot instead of going left. So I sent the second half to the right, and nobody who headed in that direction ever made it to the cemetery. Several family members called the funeral home over the next half hour to locate the grave site, and one man in particular returned in person to insist that it was our home's fault he couldn't find it. He kept saying, "Now, I am not blaming y'all, but I don't know who else's fault it could be."

After hearing that about ten times, I'd had enough. Loudly and harshly, I blurted, "Sir, you are blaming me!" He fired back, "Boy, I'll whoop you right where you stand!

Don't you get tough with me!" I snickered, wondering if he was planning to hit me over the head with his AARP membership card.

Needless to say, my dad was not thrilled. Even my mom was upset. And it pains me to confess that both of them were legitimately peeved. Tolerance back then was not my strong suit. I hadn't been seeking a way to resolve the problem so that all of us could walk away happy; instead, I'd taken a defensive stance, ready to step outside and engage in fisticuffs if needed. I clearly had a lot to learn.

Gradually things got better. One day after lunch, a gentleman came in and told me that his father was being cared for in hospice and had only a few days left. I suggested a prearrangement and filled out biographical information for the impending death certificate. We chatted for another fifteen minutes, and he agreed to call us when the time came.

A few days later when we got the notification, I was out securing a doctor's signature on another death certificate and braving the icy personality of his receptionist. (Medical receptionists generally consider people like me total nuisances.) When I returned to the funeral home, Mom told me that Dad had already left to pick up the body, but the son and his wife were waiting.

I sat down with them; discussed merchandise and services; and before I knew it, all arrangements had been completed. Everything had gone smoothly. The following day, after I'd made my usual rounds, Mom told me the gentleman had just dropped off his father's clothing and paid the bill in full. He'd also told her what a nice person I was and how calm, professional, and knowledgeable I'd been. I'd never expected that kind of a compliment so early in my career, particularly since during the entire meeting I'd been telling myself, "Don't screw this up. Give him the correct price, and calculate the sales tax accurately."

What have I learned over the years from my father? That being a renowned and respected funeral director with a sterling reputation for treating other people well requires constant effort and attention to detail. It's about far more than just working visitations, keeping up on paperwork, missing your son's baseball game, or leaving a holiday party early. It's also about compassionately helping another family from beginning to end through one of the toughest ordeals that life inevitably hands us.

Dad has also taught me that, in most cases, the customer is right. Sometimes, regardless of the business you're in, whatever you do will never be enough. So Dad has repeatedly stressed the virtue of patience and the need not to get worked up over uncontrollable variables. Patience was apparently not a gift that God ever thought Websters should have. I've had to work at it. But I've learned that with patience comes experience and with experience comes confidence.

So much of this job involves waiting. When things are slow, we wait for the phone to ring. When a death occurs, we wait for a son who lives twenty-five miles away to come to view his mom before we can carry her away. All of the puzzle pieces must line up and fit together, and some outward force is needed to push them in the right direction. In every case, once I figure out how to harness that force, then apply it appropriately, this business becomes the most rewarding, fulfilling thing I could ever imagine.

I've seen the way people greet my father at a visitation, or anywhere in public for that matter. They're so warm and friendly, so genuinely glad to see him. They really want to hear about his business and about how our family is doing. And we know they'll call us whenever the death of a loved one occurs because of the kindness and concern that my dad has always projected.

What's comical, though, is how often we are mistaken for each other. Over the phone our voices sound nearly identical. Whenever I answer with a hearty "Webster Funeral Home," the response is almost always, "Bob?"

"No. Michael."

"You sound just like him."

"I know. Please don't hold that against me."

At visitations I often hear, "Ahh, so you are Bob's boy," or, "OK, now I can put a face with the voice." Soon I hope it will be, "Hey, good to see you, Michael. You keeping that old man of yours out of trouble?"

Yes, I am—just as soon as I can find him a hobby.

ROBERT D. WEBSTER has been a licensed embalmer and funeral director in the state of Ohio since 1977. As a teenager he was initiated into the funeral home business by mowing the grass, washing the cars, and performing other menial, yet important at the time, duties that served as a springboard for his eventual chosen profession. He completed grade school, junior high, and high school in Hamilton, Ohio, and graduated from Miami University and the Cincinnati College of Mortuary Science. Upon licensure, he worked for other funeral homes in the area for twenty-four years. He opened The Webster Funeral Home in 2001 in Fairfield, Ohio.